Intimacy With God

31 Ways He Reveals His Love for Us

Intimacy With God

31 Ways He Reveals His Love for Us

CHAIM BENTORAH

Copyright © 2018 Chaim Bentorah. All rights reserved.
This book was orginially published as *God's Love for Us* Copyright © 2015

No part of this publication may be reproduced, stored, or transmitted in any form or by any means, including written, copied, or electronically, without prior written permission from the publisher. The only exception is brief quotations in printed reviews.

Short excerpts may be used with the publisher's or author's expressed written permission.

INTIMACY WITH GOD

31 Ways He Reveals His Love for Us

Cover and Interior Page design by True Potential, Inc.
ISBN: 9781948794183 (paperback)
ISBN: 9781948794190 (ebook)

True Potential
REACH THE WORLD

True Potential, Inc.
PO Box 904, Travelers Rest, SC 29690
www.truepotentialmedia.com

Produced and Printed in the United States of America.

INTRODUCTION

Genesis 2:18: "And the LORD God said, [It is] not good that the man should be alone; I will make him an help meet for him." I grew up listening to preachers quote this verse in Genesis always hearing them say that God created a woman as a helpmate. It wasn't until I was in my last year of Bible College that I actually took a close look at what I was reading in Genesis 2:18 and discovered it was not help mate but a help meet. Most of our modern translations simply say a helper or a companion. However, when I examined this word helper in the Hebrew I found that the expression in Hebrew is a suitable helper. Looking at this in its Semitic origins 'help meet' is really the Hebrew words ezer kinagado, which is literally rendered as *a helper in front of him*. Kinagado comes from the root word neged, which literally means to be before or ahead of something.

When used to modify the word ezer, which means a helper, it is a helper who goes before you, who paves the way for you, makes your journey easier. Yet a journey must have a destination. Just what is the destination that this ezer is leading man to? Within the context of this passage, it could only be a helper that is going to lead man to his final destination with God. Thus the words 'help meet' really describe why the woman was created. She was created to help man meet God. In the Babylonian Talmud Berakoth 10b Rabbi Jose B Hanina commented on II Kings 4:9. (And she said unto her husband, "Behold now, I perceive that this [is] an holy man of God, which passeth by us continually".) "You learn from this that a woman can recognize the holy character of a guest better than a man." In other words, a woman is meant to be a helper to man to aid him in spiritual understanding.

This is not only because a woman tends to be more spiritual than a man, but because she is able to give man a natural understanding of something in the supernatural. Let's go back to Genesis 2:18 and see what God does when he discovers that it was not good for man to be alone. The word in Hebrew for *alone* is *bad*. That is not the origin of our English word for *bad*; it is just a nice little coincidence that the Hebrew word for alone is *bad*. In this case, it was *bad* for Adam to be *alone*.

There is such a gulf between the natural and the supernatural. Adam was a physical being and God was a spiritual being. This created a little problem in understanding the relationship that God desired from Adam. How could God as a spiritual being explain love, intimacy, tenderness, gentleness, protectiveness, nurturing, caring, passion and longing to a natural being? I am not saying this was a problem for God; it was a problem for Adam. The only problem is that Adam did not know he had such a problem.

So we learn in Genesis 2:19: "And out of the ground the LORD God formed every beast of the field, and every fowl of the air; and brought [them] unto Adam to see what he would call them: and whatsoever Adam called every living creature, that [was] the name thereof." Now note Adam was to examine each creature and declare what he would call them and that became their name. I am not saying Adam spoke Hebrew but there is a good example in the Hebrew language, which explains what is going on here. The dog came up to Adam. We all know what it is like when we meet a friendly little dog or puppy. They smile at us, wag their tail and we just cannot resist giving the mutt a hug. So Adam called this dog kalav. Kalav then became the dog's name. The word name in Hebrew is *shem* which means reputation, what one is recognized as or noted for. Kalav in Hebrew means dog but is it spelled Kap, Lamed Vav. The Lamed Vav is the word for heart and the Kap is a preposition "as" or "like". Thus kalav in Hebrew means like your heart. Indeed a dog is like your heart, he can captivate your heart. This is what was going on in verse 19. Adam was relating his personal feelings about each animal and that feeling was expressed as their name. Note in verse 20: "And Adam gave names to all cattle, and to the fowl of the air, and to every beast of the field; but for Adam there was not found an help meet for him." The very syntax of this verse is telling us that Adam was searching for a helpmeet. He was searching for someone who could help him understand his relationship with God. Although each animal showed a certain attribute of God none could show him the most important and that is love. Oh a dog could love Adam and Adam could love the dog but they could not share an intimacy. I mean that is just too creepy to even think about.

So in the very next verse God takes the very DNA of Adam and creates another creature just like him, but yet a little different - a difference that allows the two to join together in a way that he could not join with another animal or even with another man. In that joining together and sharing that intimacy together, communicating together, sharing one's hopes and dreams together God was able to present man with an understanding of what it was that he so longed to share with man on a spiritual level that he shares on a natural level. We cannot call it sexual intercourse because that is only possible between two natural beings. But the passion, the intimacy, the love, the caring, the honesty, the oneness and the joys of that relationship are the emotions that God desires to share with us.

I recall how Rabbi Benjamin Blech in his book *The Secrets of Hebrew Words* said this: "Adam in Gematria is 45: Aleph = 1, Daleth = 4, Mem = 40. "A Father (in Hebrew 'av) is 3: Aleph = 1, Beth = 2. A mother (in Hebrew 'em) is 41: Aleph = 1, Mem = 40. Together 'av (father) and 'em 3 and 41 are 44. That is still insufficient for the uniqueness of Adam. To Mother and Father must be added one, the One of the Universe." In other words, God intended for a unity of man and woman to create a unity with Him. When God created the world he said it was good. Good in Hebrew is tov which means to be in harmony with something. When He created the world it was in harmony with Him. When He created the birds, animals and plant life they were all in harmony with Him. Yet, when He created man, He did not declare man as good. He had to add that He also created woman and then man and woman were good or in harmony with Him.

Is it any wonder that the enemy has waged such heavy warfare against the family and marriage? The enemy knows it is in the marriage and family relationship that we come to an understanding of the very nature of what the love of God really means. Thus, the enemy tries to flood us with pornography, abusive marriage relationships, adultery, and child abuse and neglect to totally distort our understanding of the love of God.

Yet throughout Scripture God continually refers to the marriage and family relationship as a natural means to express and explain His love for us. This book will examine in the original Hebrew, Aramaic, and Greek many Biblical references to marriage and the family which express the heart of God. As I continue my journey to the heart of God I find that the closer I get to the heart of God the more I am referencing the marriage and family relationship and the more I realize how the breakdown of the home and family is truly breaking the heart of God.

CONTENTS

CHAPTER 1 – THE FULLNESS OF JOY - 15

This chapter does an in-depth study of key Hebrew words in Psalms 16:11 and the joy that is found in a marriage relationship compared to the joy in a relationship with God.

CHAPTER 2 - GOD IS TAKING A RISK - 18

This chapter does a study of Song of Solomon 4:9 examining from the Hebrew the risks of love and the fact that God takes the same risk when he chooses to love us.

CHAPTER 3 - BETROTHED TO JESUS - 23

This is a study of Hosea 2:21 and explains the ancient Jewish concept of a betrothal and likens it to the relationship that God desires with us.

CHAPTER 4 - A DATE NIGHT WITH JESUS - 30

A Hebraic study is done on Psalms 17:3 explaining how observing the Sabbath should be like a married couple having a date night once a week with each other.

CHAPTER 5 – HE WILL REST IN HIS LOVE - 34

A study of keywords from Zephaniah 3:17 showing that God loves to be in love just as a young couple loves to be in love.

CHAPTER 6 - THE UNFAITHFUL LOVER - 38

In a Hebraic examination of Exodus 20:3 we discover that God feels much the same way when we seek the attention of other gods as a wife feels if her husband seeks the attention of other women.

CHAPTER 7 – A GOOD KIND OF SELFISHNESS - 42

An examination in the original Hebrew of Proverbs 16:4 reveals that God gets a special joy in making us happy just as a husband or wife receives a special joy in making their mate happy. An argument is made that there is a good kind of selfishness.

CHAPTER 8 - AND HE GAVE TO MOSES HIS BRIDE - 45

We find that when we examine Exodus 31:18 in the Hebrew that the concept of being a bride to God is found even in some of the earliest records.

CHAPTER 9 - BELOVED OF FRIEND - 50

When viewed in the original Hebrew Hosea 3:1 reveals to us that love for both a mate and God is something that does not happen overnight but is a process of growth over a period of time.

CHAPTER 10 – BRIBING GOD - 53

By looking at Malachi 3:13-14 in the Hebrew we begin to see how our church attendance, tithing, Bible study and prayer can be nothing more than a bribe to get God to bless us and is as ridiculous as a husband bringing flowers and saying sweet things to his wife to bribe her into letting him spend the weekend with his buddies. God is no more pleased with our tithes and offers given to get something in return than a wife is when her husband gives her flowers for some selfish gain.

CHAPTER 11 – ARE WE THE BRIDE OR GROOM? - 57

This chapter examines Isaiah 62:5 in the original language to explore the idea that we are not only the bride of Christ, but a husband as well. As a husband seeks to protect the heart of his wife so too we seek to protect the heart of God.

CHAPTER 12 – BRINGING PLEASURE TO GOD - 60

Psalms 90:16-17 in the original language suggest to us that just as a husband and wife are capable of bringing pleasure to each other, so too can God bring pleasure to us and us to Him.

CHAPTER 13 – CAPTIVE TO GOD'S HEART - 65

Jeremiah 3:10 suggests something in the Hebrew that we often do not consider in our relationship to God. We are really held captive to God as prisoner. Yet like the loving couple who often joke of the *old ball and chain* it is a captivity that we welcome and have no desire to escape.

CHAPTER 14 – CLEAVE TO THE LORD - 69

Genesis 2:24 tells us that a man is to cleave to his wife and then in Deuteronomy 4:4 we are instructed to cleave to God. It is the same word *devekut*. Devekut in the Jewish and ancient Semitic mindset means a whole lot more than our Christian commentaries and lexicons are telling us.

CHAPTER 15 - DELIGHTING IN GOD - 73

Psalm 37:3-4 is familiar to us all, delighting ourselves in the Lord will give us the desires of our hearts. Yet in a love relationship that tends to take on a different meaning. Consider for a moment what it means if you say that when a husband delights himself in his wife she will give him the desires of his heart. Would that change how we view this Psalms 37:3-4?

CHAPTER 16 – HE WILL TAKE US - 77

Psalms 18:16: "He sent from above, he took me, he drew me out of many waters." In studying Jewish literature I discovered that the word in Hebrew for "he took me" is the very same word used when a man declares to his friends, "I am taking myself a wife." Psalms 18:16 takes on a whole new meaning when viewed in this light.

CHAPTER 17 – FATHER - 79

Ok, we want God to be a father and cringe at the idea of giving him feminine characteristics, despite the fact that he created a woman just as much in His image as a man. Yet an examination of Psalms 103:13 in the original Hebrew suggests that a Father may not fit that completely macho image that our culture gives him.

CHAPTER 18 – GIVING GOD A HUG - 82

If a husband and wife are not in the habit of giving each other a hug, that relationship is going to suffer. Yet, if we are betrothed or married to God should not God be giving us a hug and we giving Him a hug? Does Scripture teach that we can hug God? I believe a Jewish and Hebraic understanding of Deuteronomy 10:20 teaches just that.

CHAPTER 19 – GOD LONGS TO SHARE HIS HEART - 85

We Christians are very good at pouring our hearts out to God. Yet what would a marriage relationship be like if just the wife poured out her heart to her husband but the husband never shared his heart with her? A look at keywords from Psalms 23:2, 6 in the Hebrew reveal our relationship with God is not one-sided. Just as we long to pour our heart out to Him, He also longs to pour His heart out to us. It is time to let God have His turn in sharing His heart with us.

CHAPTER 20 – GOD WANTS TO GIVE YOU A KISS - 83

We watch a movie where a handsome young man takes his lover in his arms and gives her a passionate kiss and we swoon. Yet, to suggest that the God of the Universe would take us in his arms and give us a kiss sounds almost, well creepy. Yet, if we examine the Hebrew alternative renderings in Numbers 12:8 we may find that is exactly what God longs to do with us.

CHAPTER 21 – WHEN HAROLD ABANDONED HIS DAISY - 92

Some people feel as if God has abandoned them. Harold may have felt he abandoned his Daisy, but his Daisy knew otherwise. Read Deuteronomy 31:8 in the Hebrew and discover why Harold did not abandon his Daisy and why we can know that God will never abandon us.

CHAPTER 22 – SAMSON SPOKE HIS HEART - 95

We all know from Sunday School why Samson lost his strength, it was because Delilah cut his hair. That is not what the Bible says, however. He began to lose his strength when she afflicted him. In the Hebrew, that word *afflict* can be pretty racy. But even that is not the reason God removed his presence from Samson, it was something else, something that will cause a wife to remove her presence from her husband.

CHAPTER 23 – A TRYSTING PLACE - 99

A husband and wife need a trysting place, a place where they can go off alone and not be disturbed. A place where they can freely express their love to each other without fear of being interrupted or spied upon. We need to have a similar place with God and I believe there is a word in Exodus 40:35 that would more properly be rendered as *a trysting place* with God.

CHAPTER 24 – KNOWING GOD'S THOUGHTS - 103

We wonder how we can hear the voice of God let alone know His thoughts as expressed in Isaiah 55:8. Well, consider an old married couple who have been married for many years. They can almost read each other's mind. Pay attention to these elderly couples next time you are in church, they may just teach you how you can not only hear the voice of God but know His thoughts as well.

CHAPTER 25 – GOD'S TWINKIE - 107

We have all seen them, the Twinkies, that teenage guy and his little girlfriend leaving classes at their high school, holding hands, sharing an earbud to their iPod listening to *their song*, staring in each other's eyes as if the world, the cars that go bump on the street they are crossing do not exist. It's cute, it's sweet, and it makes you sigh. Yet, if God *racham* ('s) you, you and He are Twinkies.

CHAPTER 26 - LOVE (CHAV, RACHAM) - 111

John 3:16 tells us God loves the world. John 21:20 tells us of the disciple whom Jesus loved. In the Greek both words for love are *agape*. Yet, in the Aramaic, the language that many scholars believe is the language that Jesus spoke there are two different words used for love. Does that mean that God loved this disciple more than the world? No, it means something else, something so wonderful and we Christians just miss out on the privilege that exists for us as believers.

CHAPTER 27 – JEALOUSY - 114

Oh yes, jealousy, as Shakespeare said it is the green-eyed monster which doth mock the meat it feeds upon. Actually, during Shakespeare's day, he was quite a radical to suggest such a thing about jealousy. Jealousy had a much different meaning back then and was probably more in line with the meaning of the Hebrew word *quanna* than our idea of jealousy today.

CHAPTER 28 – MAN LAYING WITH A MEMORY - 116

Alright, do I have to bring homosexuality into this book? Well, if I am to address the Hebrew secondary meanings of Leviticus 20:13 I fear I must. I must for this passage has more to say about pornography than it does about homosexuality.

CHAPTER 29 – SWEET FORBIDDEN LOVE - 120

We all know that God gave Adam and Eve forbidden fruit in the Garden of Eden and along came the enemy and persuaded them to eat of it. Yet, do you realize that the enemy also has his forbidden fruit that he will not allow God to touch? Yet God figured out a way and He is ready and able to pull the same stunt on the enemy that the enemy pulled on Him in the Garden of Eden. Find out about it when you read Song of Solomon 2:3 in the original language. Here's back at you ya ol' goat

CHAPTER 30 – TENDER EYES THE REJECTED LOVER - 123

I learned in Bible College and Seminary that Leah was crossed eyed or had some disfigurement which is why Jacob was not attracted to her. However, the Talmud and the Hebrew teach something much different.

CHAPTER 31 – THE MOST PRECIOUS THING - 126

Job 13:15 is a very popular verse but do we really know what it means? Check it out in the Hebrew and you will begin to realize what *the most precious thing* is. The Jewish Talmud gives a very delightful story to explain this verse.

CHAPTER 1 – THE FULNESS OF JOY

Psalm 16:11 Thou wilt shew me the path of life: in thy presence [is] fulness of joy; at thy right hand [there are] pleasures for evermore.

The Psalms, more than any other book in the Bible is a book which gives us an in-depth understanding of the love relationship that we can have with the God of the universe. The Psalms are written in poetry because poetry with its pictures and metaphors can best describe what a language cannot describe in ordinary words. In Edmond Rostand's play *Cyrano de Bergerac* you have the main character Cyrano who is a gifted poet and his rival for Roxane's love Christian who is a literary doofus. When each expresses their love for Roxane they express it in different ways. When Roxane asks Christian to tell her how he loves her he blurts out, "I love you a lot." When Cyrano expresses his love for Roxane he says something like: "Love grows and struggles like…an angry child…Breaking my heart…his cradle…But…such a babe is dangerous; why not have it smothered new born? And so I do… and yet he lives… I found…as you shall find…this new born babe…an infant… Hercules! Strong enough…at birth… to strangle those two serpents - Doubt and Pride. (Act 3).

As you can see, to simply say "God loves you" is meaningful but to really express it and understand what that really means one must use imagery, stories, metaphors and other poetic devices to really express the depth of that one word. I recall a young woman who was accepted into the medical school of the University of Chicago to train to be a physician. This is a very prestigious University and only the best of the best can be accepted into this school. She had an encounter with Jesus and fell in love with Him and wanted to devote her life to pursuing this love she had for Jesus and felt that her medical training would prevent her from pursuing this love relationship that she was experiencing. So she turned down the opportunity to attend this elite school which some would say would be the ultimate of the American dream to pursue her love for Jesus, perhaps as a missionary or in evangelism. Her friends and family said she was insane, crazy or brainwashed by a cult. Yet, she told of an experience where the presence of God left her briefly and after many years she has never forgotten the horror, the devastation or that lost feeling when the presence of God left her for that brief moment. She would not trade that presence of God, that love relationship with Him, for anything in the world, not even fulfilling her personal dream of attending a top medical school and becoming a physician. The love of God in Christ Jesus was far more important than anything this world had to offer. Yet unless you really experience it, how do you describe it? How do you explain such a thing so that people could understand?

God gave us a marriage/love relationship between a man and woman to help us understand in the natural why this young woman made her decision to abandon her own personal dreams. We could fill a stadium with books of love poems, stories, novels, and screenplays that have been written of individuals who have given up great dreams, hopes and plans to be with the one they love. You have in the movie Fiddler on the Roof where Tevye's daughter Hodel falls in love with a young Russian radical Perchik who is arrested and sent off to Siberia. Hodel goes to Siberia to be with him explaining that she is not going because he asked her to go, but because she wants to go, because she loves him. We see this story and no one questions this young woman's decision to leave the comforts of her home and family to experience the harshness of a Siberia work camp with the man she loves. In fact, we applaud her and we swoon over her decision and sigh over such love. Yet when a young woman gives up her dream of medical school to pursue her love for God, well she is crazy, she is brainwashed, and she is the victim of a cult. But we can love God with the intensity that any young woman can love a man or a man a woman and give up their dreams to be with their beloved. We can understand their longing to be with their beloved, we can understand the thrill and joy they experience when just hearing their lover's voice over the phone. Yet, if we claim such love for God, well, we are crazy, there is something really wrong with us. Yet God created a man and woman to be able to experience this deep love, this intimacy, this longing to help us understand what we can experience with God and more important to understand the deep love, the intimacy and the longing God has for us.

Look at Psalms 16:11: "Thou will show me the path of life." Actually, in Hebrew, it is rendered as "You cause me to know the path of life." The word for *to know* is *todi'eni* from the root word *yada'* which is an intimate knowing, but it is also in a Hiphal form so David is writing here that his love for God is *causing* him to be so intimate with God that he wants only to follow God's *path* for his life. The word *path* is not *derek* which a Hebrew student would assume, it is the word *orch* which is a *way of life*. It is that intense love of God that caused this young woman to forsake the path of education and medical training which was her desire and to pursue the *way of life* that God had chosen for her. A way which would guarantee forever His presence in her life.

Note the next part of this verse: *in thy presence [is] fullness of joy*. The word *fullness* is *soba* which is a word used to describe a feast where you eat so much that you cannot eat another bite. You can't even eat that warm, soft little brownie that the waiter puts in front of you because you are so full. That is the fullness of joy that David receives from the presence of God. The word *joy* is *simchah* which is a joy and love that a young man or woman feels where they meet their lover and takes their beloved in their arms, hugs them and kisses them. Suddenly, the world no longer exists, all that exists is just that moment in the arms of their beloved. They want that joy to go on forever. And you know what? That is exactly what God promises when He takes you in His arms and holds you close for He says: *at thy right hand [there are] pleasures for evermore*. The right hand for the majority of the people is the dominant hand and has always been the symbol of strength and power. When God takes us in His right hand He is saying that He has a grip on us that He will never let go. As he holds us we will have *na'iym* forever. Do you ever watch one of those movies where at the end the man and woman have at last found each other and in the closing scene they embrace and their lips touch each other? All of a sudden there is the most romantic music and singing in the background as the scene fades out and you sit back and sigh for this couple who will obviously live happily ever after. That word for *pleasures* is *na'iym* which means *singing and sweet sounding music*. When God takes us in his arms and embraces us in love and we return that love to him the pleasure, singing, and music of that moment is intended to go on forever.

Tell me why is it that a movie which shows a young man or woman giving up a promising career for the one they love and ends up in each other's arms filled with joy and happiness is so popular and leaves you with such a good feeling but when you hear about someone giving up a promising career for the God that she loves and loves her, we think it is craziness? God gave us those love scenes in books, movies, and poetry to help us understand that such love does exist between Him and us.

CHAPTER 2 - GOD IS TAKING A RISK

Song of Solomon 4:9: "Thou hast ravished my heart, my sister, my spouse; thou hast ravished my heart with one of thine eyes, with one chain of thy neck."

"Have you ever been in love? Horrible isn't it? It makes you so vulnerable. It opens up your heart and it means that someone can get inside and mess you up." Neil Gailman

I once had a rabbi tell me that the Song of Solomon was a very difficult book to read in Hebrew. It is difficult to read for two reasons. The book is pure poetry and as such, it is very difficult to find the right English words to match the emotion and power of the Hebrew words. It is also difficult to read because once you have been able to decipher the poetic song, your heart will break over the revelation of how much God truly loves you and longs for you and how we have so lightly treated His passion.

If we examine this passage very carefully in the Hebrew we discover something about God that very few Christians really consider and if they did they might think twice about falling into sin. Practically every modern translation you read of this verse will put a different spin on Song of Solomon 4:9. There is no literal translation and no direct link to the English language. The French or Italian language, which has poetic nature to it, can do a much better job of rendering this passage than we can do in the scientific and precise English language. But, this book is targeted to an English speaking audience so I must do the best I can with what the English language provides.

"Thou hast ravished my heart" in the Hebrew is one of the most beautiful and

at the same time heartbreaking words that I have ever run across in my 40 years of studying Biblical Hebrew. You see it is only one word in Hebrew – *livabethini*. This comes from the root word *levav* which means *heart*, but as a verb is in a piel perfect form which intensifies the word.

The first thing to note is that this is one of the rare cases where the double Beth is used. The Beth represents the heart. Some ancient rabbis have suggested that a double Beth represents God's heart and our hearts joined together in a love relationship. It is a picture of two hearts opening up to each other and becoming equally as vulnerable. Do you want to understand God's heart? Then look at your own, it was created in His image. Is not your heart wounded when someone you care about just ignores you? Do you not grieve when someone you look forward to being with calls five minutes before your time together and says: "Oh, sorry, I am too busy for you right now?" What do we do to God's heart when we ignore Him, or are too busy to spend a moment in prayer?

I found in extra-Biblical literature that the word *livabethini* is used for pulling bark from a tree. As many of us are aware, when we pull the bark from a tree, we are wounding that tree. My study partner looked up what it means to pull bark from a tree.

What she found is this: "Trees are often thought of as towering giants which are difficult to kill. Many people, however, are often surprised to find out that removing tree bark can actually harm a tree. Tree bark damage is not only unsightly but can be deadly to the tree.

For all intents and purposes, tree bark is the skin of the tree. The main tree bark function is to protect the phloem layer. The phloem layer is like our own circulatory system. It brings the energy produced by leaves to the rest of the tree." Heather Rhoades - Arboriculturist

I remember as a child how we used to go to the forest preserve and strip the bark off of trees and playfully throw it at each other, never realizing that we were hurting that tree, wounding it and possibly killing it. It's just like many Christians who playfully toy with sin never realizing that they are hurting God's heart and wounding Him, yes even to the point that His Son died on a tree.

So what is Solomon saying when he says that his beloved has *ravished his heart* or *livabethini*? He is saying that just one glance from his beloved and he has hopelessly fallen in love with her. She has stripped him of that hard shell that he built around his heart to protect it and he has made himself vulnerable to her. He is a king with the most powerful security force in the world surrounding him to protect him. Twenty elite, heavily armed, skilled warriors surround his bedchamber at night, yet one little peasant woman has the power to bring him to his knees, wound him in a way from which no bodyguard can protect him. With just a mere look or glance at him and he is caused to open his heart and say: "I am giving you the ability to break this heart, you have my heart in your hands, please be careful with it. There is no one to protect my heart from you, only you can protect it."

If we are the bride of Christ and He is our bridegroom, does it not follow that He is also saying to us: "You have ravished my heart?" When you worship Him, you look up to heaven with that love in your eyes and you have caused God to rip the bark from His heart as He says to you: "I may be God, a towering giant to you that seems invulnerable, but I am stripping my bark off the tree of my heart, I am exposing myself to you, I am making myself vulnerable to you, I am giving you my heart. You have the ability to deeply wound my heart, no one but you can protect it, please be gentle with my heart."

How many of us have broken the heart of God? How many of us have bowed to the temptation of sin thinking no one is getting hurt. Yet the one who loves you the most is the one who is being hurt. He is the one who is left with the broken heart after you have prostituted your love with the other gods of this world.

Is it any wonder that we have a God who can truly feel an empathy for us when our hearts are broken? Look at Psalms 34:18 "*The LORD [is] nigh unto them that are of a broken heart; and saveth such as be of a contrite spirit.*"

I once had an orthodox rabbi tell me, "You Christians, you do not understand the heart of David, you are so one dimensional." Indeed we are, for we automatically assume that the expression of a *broken heart* means only one thing and we never seek to examine the dynamics of a broken heart when it comes from the lips of David. Practically every modern translation will render *lenisheveri* as *broken*. This gives the impression that God's love is somehow special to those who have suffered a wounded heart. Although such a thought can be of great comfort during a time of brokenness, I believe there is something much deeper that David is trying to express.

Most modern translations use the KJV as a model for their translations and as such, they often move in lockstep with old and established renderings that have been endeared by Christians throughout the centuries. Although the rendering of *broken heart* is fully appropriate, it does not allow for the ambiguity of the text. My brother gave me some notes published by Wycliffe Bible Translators to assist me with my doctoral dissertation. In that, I read a statement from a former professor at Dallas Seminary who is now on staff with Yale University. He said that many of our modern translations often reflect the doctrine of the particular denomination or church that the translator represents. In translating it is important to retain the ambiguity of many Hebrew words in one's renderings so that the reader will have the freedom to allow the Spirit of God to speak to him in ways that the teachings of his particular church would limit.

Lenisheveri lev is the perfect example. By rendering this as *broken heart* to stay with tradition we limit what the Holy Spirit can reveal to us personally. *Broken heart* is not a mistranslation or incorrect translation, it is just a limiting translation for these words express so much more of what was going on in David's heart. *Lenisheveri (broken)* comes from the root word *shavar*. The Lamed before the word is a preposition and the Nun indicates that it is in a Niphal form. Rather than limiting our range of renderings it only broadness it and gives the Holy Spirit a lot of leverage to speak to the hearts of men.

One possible rendering for *shavar (broken)* is a *breakthrough*. The Lord is near to those who are experiencing a breakthrough in their hearts. A broken heart is often an opportunity for a *breakthrough* in one's heart. You often hear about *rebounding* after a couple breaks up. People are often advised to wait a period of time before starting a new relationship as your heart is very tender after a breakup and you may seek to fill that emptiness with another relationship too quickly and end up making a serious mistake. Of course, what better person to catch on a rebound than Jesus. He is the perfect one to rebound to for He fully understands the dynamics of your brokenness for He Himself has suffered a broken heart and as He is perfect in his empathy He will carefully guard your heart as you rest in his loving arms.

David knew that when his heart was broken there was another suitor, God, waiting at the door. When his other *gods (lust, wealth, power, advisers, friends, etc.)* failed him, God was there waiting for his chance to capture David's heart. David saw his *broken heart* as an opportunity. As a wound, when healing, is very tender to the touch his wounded heart would be very tender to the touch of God and would feel God's touch in a way he would never feel that touch prior to his loss.

You see David had a heart after God's heart. This did not only mean he understood God's heart but that his heart was constantly seeking to be joined with the heart of God. Hence, every wound he felt, every rose in his life that died, was an opportunity to experience the touch of God in a way he could not experience when all was well in his life, when every rose in his life was in bloom and healthy.

When that *rose* in your life fades or dies and you are left with a broken heart, what do you do? You weep, you mourn, and you express your sorrow in many different ways. These are normal responses and grieving must be allowed, but don't let that wound blind you to the fact that there is another suitor who is waiting at the door. One that you can rebound to, who will love you, hold you, embrace you, speak tenderly to you and protect your heart. He is ready to seize the opportunity to touch your wounded heart and, like David, you can welcome your *lenisheveri lev (broken heart)* as an opportunity, a *breakthrough,* to feel the touch of God in a way you could never feel it when your *rose* was in full bloom. When you suffer a broken heart you just want to be alone. Ok, be alone, but maybe just maybe you would be willing to open the door of your heart a crack to let in that other Suitor who has also suffered a broken heart after having made Himself vulnerable to one He loved and had that love betrayed. Who knows better how to treat a broken heart than one who has also suffered a broken heart?

CHAPTER 3 - BETROTHED TO JESUS

Hosea 2:21, "And I will betroth thee unto me forever; yea, I will betroth thee unto me in righteousness, and in judgment, and in lovingkindness, and in mercies."

It is interesting that in the Book of Hosea God likens Israel to a woman who is betrothed. The word in Hebrew for betrothed is 'eras which your lexicon will tell you means either betrothed or to be engaged for matrimony. It comes from the same root as earth or land and in its Semitic root has the idea of building a foundation. The betrothal period between a man and woman is where we get our modern day idea of an engagement. The idea is to spend some time building a foundation to your relationship before you actually take on the vows of marriage and enter into a physical intimacy. The term betrothal in Jewish law must not be understood in our modern sense, that is in the sense of a man and woman form an agreement to marry but they are not yet legally bound and at any time that agreement can be broken or dissolved without any legal consequence. This idea is not what is found in the Bible for the word betrothal as this practice came about in the Middle Ages and modern times. Yet the Talmud gives a very different view of betrothal. The Talmudic definition of a betrothal is to contract an actual though incomplete marriage. In fact, you will find two examples in Scripture where a wife is considered a betrothed. II Samuel 3:14: "My wife whom I have betrothed *('erasti – my betrothed)*. The second example is Deuteronomy 22:24: the betrothed is designated as the *wife of his neighbor*. Rabbinical law declares that the betrothal is equivalent to an actual marriage and can only be dissolved by divorce.

A betrothal period of twelve months is allowed to pass before the marriage was completed by the formal home-taking – nissu'in likkuhin. If the bride and groom were widowed the period was reduced to thirty days. It was at this time that the bride and groom would consummate their union physically for the first time. In other words, they were not allowed to have a sexual relationship for twelve months after being officially married. Often the family would provide for the couple so the groom would not have to work for that year and he would be able to spend all his time with his bride getting to know her and she him. It is during this time that they would fall in love and as the twelve months would reach its conclusion it is believed that the bridegroom could contain himself no longer, being so desirous of becoming one with his bride that at any time he would sneak out of his house, go to the house of his bride's father at night and snatch her away and take her to his home to consummate their marriage. Of course, everyone is anticipating this moment and as the bridegroom makes his way to his bride's home he is followed by many others with lit candles to help him find his way. The bride, of course, is just as anxious for her bridegroom and she is waiting for the day when her bridegroom will come. She is so certain that he could come at any moment that she will make sure she has plenty of oil in her lamp so it is lit when her bridegroom comes to take her away.

If she and her friends or bridesmaids do not have oil in her lamp or a lamp ready it was a sign that she or her bridesmaids were not interested in consummating the marriage with her bridegroom. Not that the marriage would not take place, but the bridegroom would indeed be disappointed and broken-hearted, if even one of the bride's friends had an unlit lamp.

Is this not a picture of our salvation experience? Our marriage with Jesus will not be consummated until he returns to take us to the marriage supper of the lamb. Yet, we are legally married to Jesus when we accept Him as our Savior.

Marriage and the betrothal period are a legal binding contract. The laws of a contract have not changed even to this day. To have a contract you must have an offer. The bridegroom gives an offer of marriage. Just as the Holy Spirit is giving the offer to us to be married to Jesus. The next condition to a contract is acceptance. The bride or in some cultures her father accepts the offer. Needless to say, someone must accept the offer. When we accept Jesus as our Savior we are accepting His offer to be betrothed to Him. There is a third matter to this contract called *consideration*. Most people are not aware of this. But for a contract to be binding both parties must receive some benefit. Years ago on the back of comic books, there would be an offer of five or more record albums for only one cent. People often wonder why you had to pay a penny, they were obviously giving the albums away to induce you to buy more albums. To receive your five albums you needed to sign your name on the little form at the bottom. That signature was proof that you were accepting their offer. The penny was the consideration. The company would benefit by one penny and you would benefit by receiving five record albums. That penny was enough to make a binding contract so they could keep sending you albums that you were under obligation to either purchase or send back. Of course in the laws of our land, a minor could not legally enter into a binding contract and that made up the bulk of the orders the company received, which may explain why we do not see such underhanded moves today.

So a groom gives an offer of marriage, the bride accepts but there must be a consideration to bind this marriage contract. That consideration has taken on the form of a ring as a token of the consideration. It is not the rings that are the consideration but what they represent. The consideration is that the groom will give his life to his bride and she will give her life to her husband. They belong to each other, lock, stock and barrel. I know in our culture we don't like to think of being owned by anyone, but in reality that is exactly what you are doing when you make that marriage contract. Of course, you are so in love you do not only not care that you are giving your life away to this person you are so in love with, but you actually want to do it.

When Jesus sends out his offer of marriage or betrothal to us and we accept that offer we must also realize that for this matter of salvation to become a binding contract there must be a consideration. What Jesus gives to us is His life and in return, we give Him our lives. He gives us His heart and in return, we give Him our hearts. Our lives and our hearts are no longer just ours, they belong to Jesus, just as His life and heart no longer belong to just Him but they belong to us.

So what are we going to do with this Life and Heart of Jesus that we have now been legally given? We have a heart that can easily be broken if we cheat on it, if we sleep with other gods, if we abandon it for our own purposes and desires. The results are the same as in any marriage, the offended party is heartbroken, shattered and wounded.

We are only in the betrothal stage of our relationship with Jesus while we are here on the earth. The marriage is not complete, but it is a real marriage and as we anxiously await for our bridegroom we are or should be doing what any bride is doing, preparing ourselves for our bridegroom. We are adorning ourselves, making ourselves beautiful for our bridegroom. We are learning all we can about our bridegroom so we can bring joy to His heart. Just as in that betrothal period where the bride and bridegroom just concentrate all their efforts on building their relationship, we are to spend all our time here on earth preparing for one thing: building our relationship so that when our bridegroom appears we are anxiously awaiting with oil in our lamps and an open heart to receive Him.

There is much talk among Christians today of being the bride of Christ and being married to Christ. This is, of course, a very Biblical picture of our relationship to Christ. Many Christians see the Song of Solomon as a picture of our relationship to Christ which is a story of the love relationship between King Solomon and the Shulamite woman. This is not only a Christian concept but a very Jewish concept. I read a story in Jewish literature about a rabbi who would literally dress up in a wedding outfit on the Sabbath in anticipation of the coming of the Messiah to receive him as his bride.

This is such a strong and beautiful image of our relationship with God that the enemy seeks to strike at the very heart and core of the marriage relationship today and seeks to pervert it with the many sexual pornographic perversions that exist today. He seeks to fill the sacred marriage with adultery, unfaithfulness, selfishness and turn marriage into something that becomes almost a mockery to totally distort the very picture God has given us to understand our relationship to Him.

Yet, marriage is still very popular. Stories about romance sell in novels, movies, and tabloid magazines. As some famous movie star enters her fifth marriage we all grab the latest edition of *People Magazine* to find out if she has now found her true romantic partner. We will fill a movie theater to capacity to watch a story of a man and woman who finds true love and enters a life of living happily ever after together. Our hearts are warmed as we watch an elderly couple celebrate their 60th wedding anniversary holding hands and giving each other a little kiss on the lips. Oh, how the enemy hates that because he knows we will logically look at that and begin to compare this tenderness, faithfulness, this caring, to our relationship to God. For God did give us the marriage relationship, this love relationship between a man and a woman, as a picture of our relationship to Him.

Yet keep in mind that the Bible seems to only speak of our betrothal to God as we find in Hosea and the Book of the Song of Solomon. The only time it references being married to God is when Jesus comes to take us to heaven. Apparently, the picture or image that Scripture gives us is that while on earth we are merely in a betrothal period. Jesus even alludes to the fact that while on earth we are merely in a betrothal stage in John 14:2, "In my Father's house are many rooms: if [it were] not [so], I would have told you. I go to prepare a place for you." During the betrothal period, a bridegroom spent that time building a new room or addition to his father's house where he would one day move in with his bride. Here Jesus is giving us a beautiful Semitic picture of being betrothed to us by saying He is building a room onto His father's house and when it is finished he will come and take us, His bride, away from our present world to live in His world. This is the same picture of a bridegroom who will come to take his bride from the world of her family to live in the world of his family.

So what about this word 'aras which we render as *betrothal?* It would be wrong to render it an engagement for, as explained, this is a reference to an actual marriage that is not yet consummated. The word itself 'aras comes from a Semitic root found in the Sumerian language which means *to desire*. Hence the whole idea behind a betrothal is to build a *desire between a man and woman*. I recall when I played high school football during our workouts in the hot sun. You would grow so thirsty that all you could think about was when that manager would bring out the buckets of water. Then when the water did come out the coach would torment us with more practice until we had everything the way he wanted before we could get a drink of that water. We had one guy who would start talking about a tall clear glass of water, filled with ice, frost on the side of the glass and we would be so tormented with thirst and desire for water that I actually called out in front of the whole team, "Lord send Lazarus down that he may dip his finger in some water and place it upon my tongue." There was no separation of church and state in that prayer spoken on the grounds of a public school. You tend to desire something so much more when you have it right in front of you but you are not allowed to partake of it. You know what I mean. On Thanksgiving when that feast is right in front of you, you smell it, you are starved for it, but you cannot partake of it until everyone around table says what they are thankful for. I can tell you what I am not thankful for at that moment. Then you must endure Dr. Rev. Pastor Uncle Harry as he preaches a whole sermon in saying what should be just a quick blessing over the meal. By the time mashed potatoes and gravy hit your plate your desires are so worked up it is all you can do to wait until everyone is served and the host picks up her fork before you can dive into your meal. By that time you have already covertly popped a few olives and baby sweet pickles in your mouth and may have even managed to polish off a devils egg.

Is that the desire that you find building in you as you await your Bridegroom Jesus? As I write this it is now my birthday, I am another year older. I could bemoan the fact that I am quickly approaching the final stop at the train station. I am getting older and this life here is drawing into its final stages. But for me, as with any believer we have a Bridegroom Jesus who is waiting for us at the final terminal to pick us up and carry us away to His Father's house and betroth us to Himself forever.

There was the ancient teaching that when a male child was born his soul was split in two and the other half of his soul was placed by God into a female child who would one day be born. God would anoint a *shidduch* or *matchmaker* who would have a prophetic gift to determine the young woman who had the other half of the soul of a male. Hence the term *soul mates*. Often this determination was made between two individuals who had never met each other. It was understood that there must be a period of time for these two to learn to love each other before the marriage was consummated. Thus, the Jews created this time of a betrothal. This is where the idea of an engagement originated. This whole idea of an engagement and engagement ring has its roots in Judaism. I believe that this is significant that it is a Jewish concept as God is giving us a picture of our relationship to Him.

Although Eastern Oriental culture had great taboos on a man touching or looking at a woman, when a man was betrothed, much liberty was granted for him to touch his betrothed. They would be allowed to go off into the wilderness and share their intimate thoughts and dreams and they could hold hands and exchange a kiss or two, but they could go no further. If the man and woman did engage in sex then they were officially married. In fact, the betrothal begins with a wedding ceremony where they are legally married but do not live together or engage in marital sex.

The betrothal period can be a very romantic time, a time of two lovers dreaming together, experiencing the joy of learning to commit to each other and experiencing the thrill of the touch and the nearness of one to whom they would one day become intimate in the deepest way. Usually, after a year of this, the bridegroom and bride become so *'aras (desire, betrothal)* so desirous of being intimate with each other that they begin to share their hearts with each other.

Too often in today's society, they allow the physical relationship to take place before sharing their hearts with each other. Yet in sharing their hearts with each other they are creating a bond of trust and unity so that when they do enter into a physical relationship, they will really *yada'*. The word *yada'* in Hebrew is a word used to express a knowing, but it is also used to express a man and woman who have a sexual relationship because a true, fulfilling sexual relationship cannot take place until that couple really knows each other, knows their deep hidden secrets, their desires, their longings and their dreams. They know things about each other that no one else in the world knows. That relationship is built on complete honesty with no hidden secrets.

Psalms 25:14: *"The secret of the LORD [is] with them that fear him."* During the betrothal period, the young man and woman begin to grow in their love and trust with each other that they begin to share the secrets of their hearts with each other. So too in our relationship with God. As we grow to know and love Him He will begin to share the secrets of his heart with us. That word fear does not mean to be afraid of God. A man is not afraid of his wife, but what he does fear is that he may do something to wound her heart, to break her heart. He would rather face torture and death before he would bring any harm to the heart of his beloved. A little more than a hundred years ago a gentleman would challenge another man to a duel which could result in a deep wound or even death if that challenged man should in any way offend the heart of the woman that the gentleman loved.

Indeed that word fear yara' in Hebrew must be understood within its context. In extra-Biblical literature it is often found to not be a fear for one's own safety but a fear for the safety of another. Thus, to those who fear wounding or breaking God's heart, He will reveal his secrets. Just as a husband will desire to know the secrets of his wife's heart so he will know what to do to avoid wounding her heart or breaking her heart.

During our betrothal time here on earth as we grow closer and closer to God and He begins to trust us more and more to protect His heart, He will begin to reveal His heart to us and we will begin to know just what it is that will bring joy to His heart and how to protect His heart so we will not wound it or break it.

CHAPTER 4 - A DATE NIGHT WITH JESUS

Psalms 17:3 "Thou has proved mine heart; thou hast visited me in the night."

The above passage was taken from the KJV. It translates the phrase *"thou hast visited me in the night"* in a perfect tense (completed action). I checked through every translation I could find and practically all of them translate this in the past tense. Is it just me or am I the only Christian who has ever celebrated a Sabbath evening with an orthodox Jewish family? I tend to think not. If you have ever celebrated the Sabbath evening with an orthodox family you will notice they leave their doors open during the Sabbath night prayers (or pray facing a door) to welcome the Shabbat Hamalka, the Sabbath Queen or Bride.

In the Talmud, the Shabbat is compared esoterically to a bride given to us by God, whom we long for her arrival (Shabbat 119a). Orthodox Jews don't like to tell us Christians about that because they know what we will do with it. I know what this Christian will do it with; I will immediately make an application of a visit from the Sabbath Bride to Jesus.

But let's take a look at Psalms 17:3. *"Thou hast proved mine heart."* The word for *proved* is also in a perfect tense (completed action) from the root word *bachan* which literally means a *watchtower*. In a sense, a watchtower is built so someone can look out over the land and *prove or test* his senses to determine if there is an enemy lurking around. Yeah, I know, that is stretching it to get the idea of testing from a watchtower, but translators do that and it is appropriate. However, do we really need to make such a stretch, why not simply call it a watchtower, someone to provide protection or to guard over a city? Hence this passage could be rendered:

Intimacy With God

"Thou has *guarded or protected* my heart. More literally, "Thou has been a watchtower over my heart."

Why does God *guard* or is a *watchtower* over the heart of David? So he can visit him in the night. This is where the Talmud gets the idea that what David is referring to in Psalms 17:3 is a visit from the *Sabbath Bride.* This is a depiction of the feminine side of God. What the Talmud is trying to teach here is that we are encouraged to call upon God every day, but only once a week, the Sabbath, are we allowed to be in His presence. Sure, we are in God's presence every day, but the Sabbath is meant to be a special day to be in His presence. A husband and wife may see each other every day and be in each other's presence every day, but many couples will set one evening apart for a *date night.* A special night where they are not only together, but they forget all the problems of the day, they forget all their financial problems, problems in raising their children, struggles in maintaining a home and for one evening this time in each other's presence they just focus on each other, like young lovers and enjoy just being with each other, doing special things, things they enjoy. Such a practice can only be healthy for a marriage relationship. Just as such a practice with God, to spend one day in each other's presence in a special way can only benefit in one's relationship with God.

Imagine just getting married and then having your bride go out on a business trip for 6 days a week. You make sure your presence is known to each other, you text each other tender little things like, "How's my boopsie girl?" Or you send emails relating to matters of business like, "Did you pay the electric bill?" You will even call each other and talk, making your presence known to each other. Yet, you can bet you will not use that one day when you are together at home to mow the lawn or fix the roof. And you can bet you will spend the entire six days mowing the lawn and fixing the roof to prepare for the one day you will be in your bride's presence. That is the sort of expectation that the Sabbath was meant to create. For six days we work in God's presence, we send him little messages like, "Sure need your help here, Lord," or "How am I going to pay this electric bill?" You may even send up little messages of praise and adoration during this time. But on the one day you call your *date night or Sabbath* you lay all these problems and struggles aside and you and Jesus just have a date night where you just focus on each other, hold each and simply enjoy being together.

Some Hebrew scholars suggest that the word *visit pakad* is really in a *prophetic perfect tense.* Only in recent years have Christian Hebrew scholars began to accept the fact that there is *a prophetic perfect* in the Hebrew, which is probably why it is not evident in most translations. Admittedly there are still many holdouts who claim there is no such thing as a prophetic perfect just as they will claim there is no such thing as a paragogic in the Hebrew. However, I am inclined to believe the prophetic perfect does exist in the Hebrew. In a prophetic perfect we are speaking of an event that has not yet occurred as if it has already occurred.

The word for visit is *pakad* which literally means *to visit*, but has the idea of *watch care (fits the watchtower idea), to nurture, to lie with*, as well as all sorts of other good things. So this visit is just not a "howdy do, thought I'd just drop over and watch the super bowl with you" type of visit. It is a *visit that provides protection.* If this is indeed in a prophetic perfect tense, then what David is saying is that the Lord will visit him or provide protection but he is so convinced that this is done as God does not live in time and for God the event has already taken place such that David is saying God has visited Him or protected him even before it has happened. It might be that David is filled with such anticipation of being in the presence of God on this *date night* that he is actually feeling the joy of the *date night* as he anticipates it.

It is odd here that the bride is doing the protection. How does a bride protect her husband? In ancient times as even today, a bride can protect her husband by fulfilling such needs that he will not be moved to lust, adultery, nasty little websites etc. A bride can protect her husband from sin. This is the protection that David received from God. God watching his heart and then visiting him in the night, the Sabbath Night, where God satisfies his needs and longings so he will not fall into sin. When one is satisfied with his bride, then money, fame, accomplishments and all the trappings of the world, mean nothing. The world has little to entice us when we are totally satisfied in our *bride Jesus.*

How many Hollywood movies have you seen where a man and woman marry and are dirt poor but just happy to be with each other? Then fame and fortune enter their lives and the husband and wife grow apart from each other. When they finally confront the problems in their relationship the husband will wave his hand at their mansion, swimming pool, cars, and the trappings wealth and say; "But I am working all these hours so you can have all these things." The wife then answers, "But I don't want those things, I just want you."

Is your betrothal to God just so you can get all the goodies He has to offer? Will you still love Him if He never answers another prayer, if he will never make you prosperous, give you good health or provide you with things? Is it all the benefits of being betrothed to God that you seek or is it just Him?

I spoke with a woman who had been married for over twenty years. The first seven years of their marriage was, as she described it, the *Little House on the Prairie.* Then her husband fell into alcohol and drugs, became abusive, inattentive and other things which would destroy a marriage. Yet she still remained married to him. She could have left this man. She had a good job, her kids were now grown, and she could do well on her own. She was still very attractive and would attract the attention of men, she could find someone else quite easily. I asked her "what is the benefit you are receiving in being married to him?" She said for many years there was no benefit, just a lot of pain and rejection. I then asked the obvious question, "Why are you staying married to him?" She replied, "I guess I still love him. I married him in sickness and in health, for richer or poorer for better or for worse. This is the worst, but I married him for that too."

I have met many former Christians who said they left Christianity because it just did not work for them. They were receiving no benefit. But when we entered into our betrothal with Jesus there was no guarantee that we would have a wonderful, prosperous and peaceful life. We married him for better or for worse and if the worse comes we will stick it out with Him, because we love Him.

This woman told me something else, something that keeps her going and it was hope. Hope that one day they would again have the *Little House on the Prairie*. Read Hosea 2, you will find God has the same hope in us. Although we have run off with other gods, we have broken His heart, He still longs for us. Look at Hosea 2:13-16:

Hosea 2:13 "And I will visit upon her the days of Baalim, wherein she burned incense to them, and she decked herself with her earrings and her jewels, and she went after her lovers, and forgat me, saith the LORD. Therefore, behold, I will allure her, and bring her into the wilderness, and speak comfortably unto her. And I will give her vineyards from thence, and the valley of Achor for a door of hope: and she shall sing there, as in the days of her youth, and as in the day when she came up out of the land of Egypt. And it shall be at that day, saith the LORD [that] thou shalt call me Ishi; and shalt call me no more Baali.

What does that sound like to you? It sounds to me like a God who is like my friend who has a husband that has wandered away. It sounds like my friend who is hoping for that day when they can return to the day of their youth when they were so in love and they would wander away together and speak tender things to each other. A day when they used to sing and dance together and life was so sweet and love was so strong. This is what God is so longing with us, to return to those days when we were new believers and would rejoice in every song we sang to Him and filled our days with prayers and rejoicing in Him. God is just longing for that *date night* with us.

CHAPTER 5 – HE WILL REST IN HIS LOVE

Zephaniah 3:17: "The Lord your God in the midst of you is mighty. He will save, He will rejoice over you with joy. He will rest in his love, He will joy over you with singing.

I am convinced that every born again believer longs deep within their soul and spirit to love God with all their heart soul and might. We know and understand what love is. We were made in the image of God. That word image *tselem* does not have to mean a mirror image or likeness in a physical sense but it could also be a reference to the nature and emotional makeup of someone. God is a spirit. A spirit does not have two arms, two legs, two eyes etc. A spirit has no resemblance to the corporal being of a physical person. Thus we would have to render the word *tselem* as a reference to the nonphysical makeup God which is *His heart and His longings or desires*. The greatest desire and longing of God would also be the greatest longing and desire of a human being and that is the longing to be loved. The very nature of love itself involves an act of free will. In other words, God could have programmed us to love Him but then that would not be love. God had to give us a free will so we could choose to love Him. Then he had to allow for the existence of a rival so to speak so that we would have to choose between Him and the rival.

I used to perform many marriages when I was in the ministry. So much of the joy I observed in a marriage ceremony was that the bride and groom chose to love their mate. Of all the people in the world, that person chose to love one particular person in that special way to want to commit their lives to that individual. God created each of us with the ability to love. But that love will lie dormant in us until someone comes along to awaken that love in us and then when they do that love flows out of us and begins to sing.

In Zephaniah 3:17 we learn that God will *rest in His love yacharish bi'ahavati*. These words have been very troubling for translators. To translate it in its proper syntax just flies in the face of conventional Christian thought. Yet, it may actually confirm what a believer really believes in his heart.

The word *yacharish* comes from the root word *charash* and is usually rendered as *rest*. Yet there are secondary and alternative renderings that we may consider. One alternative is something that a translator would never dare to use in this passage, yet, if you think about it, it makes perfect sense. I find that the standard rendering *He will rest in His love* really disrupts the literary flow of this passage. However, if we use another English word for *charash* it would really make more sense. That word is *enchantment*. Another word applied to *charash* is *bewitched*. Actually, we really have no English word to use which expresses the true nature of *charash*. I know such terms are very anti-God but stop and consider the use of that word in our language in a non-mystical sense. I watched two Twinkies the other day walk out their high school building after classes. It was so cute, two little teenagers holding hands, staring into each other's eyes, sharing an earplug to their iPod listening to their song together. They looked so *charash, enchanted or bewitched* with each other. Of course, there was no witchcraft involved here or any enchantment in a literal sense, we would mean it in the sense that they were just so captivated with each other with joyous feelings and contented being in each other's presence. Look at this phrase *The Lord your God in the midst of you.* That word *midst* is *karav* and means your *innermost parts, being or your heart*. When the Lord enters your heart He is *mighty* or He is empowered to save you. That power is like a running generator. It has a lot of power but until you plug something into it, that power is not being used. Until God connects with your heart, His power is not being used, His joy cannot be released.

Now note what follows, *he will rejoice over you with joy, He will rest in His love, He will joy over you with singing.* Think about it, how does *"rest in His love"* fit between those two phrases? Now plug in the English word *enchantment* as we use it in the context of these two Twinkies. *He will be enchanted with His love.* What happens when a man and woman kiss for the first time and tell each other *"I love you?"* That rush, that high, that ecstasy that is *charash*. When a woman is pregnant she loves the child within her. But after giving birth and the nurse puts that baby in the mother's arms and she sees it for the first time, what she feels is *charash*.

When you invite God into your *midst karav* or *your heart* you feel a real rush, a *charash*. But soft, what Zephaniah is telling us is that *God will charash in His love*. In other words what God also feels is *charash* that rush of *joy and enchantment* like we feel. When we invite Him into our hearts and He has our hearts completely He feels *charash*. Just like two lovers who express their love for each other, they experience a real high, not so much in receiving love from their beloved but a rush or high in having their own love for that person awakened. They then walk around like those Twinkies in a haze or a cloud, they are in love, and they are *enchanted*. But, until the object of their affection shares a mutual love, the feelings of being in love cannot be awakened. God does not stand back in smug satisfaction over our rejoicing, He is right there dancing in joy with us.

I spoke with another Christian the other day. She told how when she was first saved, she felt this rush of joy and just went around singing, happy, and filled with excitement. She ran around the church and everyone was dancing and singing with her rejoicing. As she related this I could see that joy in her face, the brightness in her eyes as she recalled that time she fell in love with Jesus. I reflected Zephaniah 3:17 and thought, "You know, I will bet the same thing was happening in heaven." Luke 15:10: *"Likewise, I say unto you, there is joy in the presence of the angels of God over one sinner that repenteth."* I began to picture Jesus gathering the angels around Him and saying: "I have taken myself a bride." In the tradition of any wedding, everyone is happy, singing and dancing and I pictured Jesus in the midst of all the angels also dancing around as this woman danced around with all her new brothers and sisters in the Lord.

You see, that is why he needs us to voluntarily give Him our hearts. That is why He gave us a free will so we can choose Him over all the other gods in this world who are out courting us. In our lifetime we have many suitor gods lining up at our doorway seeking out love. There is the suitor of wealth, power, fame, security and then there is God waiting patiently in line longing that we will choose Him over all the other gods seeking our attention. When we choose to love God over all the other gods, we fulfill or complete that love He has for us. Then God is like that Twinkie, He is in love and he likes and longs to be *in love* just like two people long to be in love and experience love. Every time someone gives their heart to God, He *rests* or *charash,* is enchanted, with His love.

Christians are saying all the time, "I want more of God, I want to feel His presence" when all the time God is saying: "I want more of you, I want to feel your presence." When you give Him all of your heart, you give Him the chance to feel the joy of being in love. Like a mother will rejoice over her baby and cherish and protect her beloved baby with her life or a husband will rejoice over his beloved wife and will cherish and protect his beloved wife with his life, so will God cherish and protect you when He is allowed to have your whole heart and he can *rest in His love* or *rejoice over being in Love.*

I believe Christians in this Western world have been so inundated with teachings that God wants to make you prosperous, heal you, bless you, give you all sorts of goodies like some sort of genie out of the bottle that our love becomes completely one-sided. Yet deep in the heart of every believer is the longing to bring some joy or some pleasure to This God who is so giving. It is so easy to do but we are so used to just coming to God with a handful of *'gimmie's' and a mouth of 'much oblige'* that we never stop to just simply say to God, *"I love you"* and allow Him to rejoice in that love and begin to sing His love song to us. We are too busy asking God to bring sunshine to our hearts that we forget to bring some sunshine to His heart.

CHAPTER 6 - THE UNFAITHFUL LOVER

Exodus 20:3 "Thou shalt have no other *(another)* gods before me."

A man came to a rabbi and asked if the rabbi could teach him the deep mysteries of God. The rabbi asked the man a question. Two burglars entered a house through a chimney. Upon emerging from the chimney one burglar had a dirty face and the other a clean face. Which one washed his face? The man quickly responded that the one with the dirty face. The rabbi replied that this showed that the man was not ready to study the deeper things of God because he could not correctly answer a simple question. The man with the clean face would have washed his face because seeing his partner had a dirty face he would have assumed his face was dirty. The one with the dirty face would not have washed his face for seeing his partner with a clean face he would have assumed his face was clean. The man replied that he now understood the depth of thinking he needed to study the deeper things of God. The rabbi replied that he did not understand the proper thinking, for how could two men come down a chimney and only one has a dirty face? Sometimes even if we are able to grasp the obvious, there is something even more obvious that we never consider. Such is the case with Exodus 20:3.

There are few people reading Exodus 20:3 who have never heard this commandment. Yet, how many have ever thought to think about what it really means?

There are three words in this passage that we need to look at closely. The first is the word *other*. In Hebrew, this is the word *'achar* which is often rendered as *another*. At first glance, the phrase: "Thou shalt have no other gods" appears similar to the phrase: "Thou shalt not have another god." The phrases are identical, except that we are so used to hearing the first phrase that we never consider its implications. Saying it a different way: "Thou shalt not have another god…" does make one think on this a little deeper because, how many times do we approach God while having another god fill our thoughts?

How many women see their husband eyeing another woman and then later that night during that time in intimacy she questions if she is really the woman that her husband is thinking about. She can sense in a very subtle way that something is not right, her husband may not have committed an outright act of adultery, but he has a roving eye and somehow she just does not feel that she is her husband's one and only and that hurts, that breaks her heart.

Do we not do the same with God? We are filled with desires for other gods and we come to God to worship Him, fulfill our duty to God and maybe He might even see fit to give us a little blessing. Yet in our minds are these other gods that we are lusting after and like that little wife lying by her husband with a broken heart, our God too weeps with a broken heart over our unfaithfulness.

The word *gods* is *Elohim*. Here is where we tend to miss the fine point of this commandment. We automatically think this is a reference to something supernatural. Since we do not worship Baal, or Zeus, or other supernatural gods, we chalk this commandment up to one that we will never break. Yet, the word *Elohim* means much more than this. An *Elohim* is anything or anyone that you put your trust in. It is anything or anyone that you depend upon for your security or build your life upon. Hence you shall not put your trust in anything *before God Jehovah*. A god does not have to be some pagan deity. It can be a simple thing like your 401K or your job. I read something written by a prophetic teacher, Rick Joyner who put it in words that make more sense than the words I could use. "If you are a sincere seeker of truth, a simple test will determine whether you are building your life on a true faith in God or in this present world. Ask yourself: 'Where do I get my encouragement, or discouragement, from?' Does it depress you when the stock market takes jolt or when you hear other troubling economic news? If we are troubled when the world begins to shake, it is a revelation of what we have been building our lives on."

So, if we look at it in this context, this would define what a *god* is. It is whatever you build your life upon.

The word *before* is *pani*. It is the word we use for *face* as well as for *the presence of God*. So literally what this verse *"Thou shalt have no other (another) gods before me"* is really saying in plain English is this: "You shall not trust in anything or person when in My Presence." The children of Israel knew all about the presence of God. It was there as a cloud by day and as a pillar of fire by night. For many of us, the presence of God is expressed in different ways. Often it is a sense of peace. Yet, if we build our lives on our jobs, our 401Ks or our money market accounts and we are stressed out over fear of losing our job or our money market accounts taking another hit, we will not enter that peace of God or his presence. To try and enter into the presence of God while fretting over our job or money market accounts would be like a man trying to be intimate with his wife while worrying over his relationship with a mistress. No man can serve two masters. Exodus 20:3 should alert us to really give serious thought as to who our real master is. Ok that is pretty obvious.

Remember the second question of the rabbis' story – how could two men come down a chimney and only one has a dirty face? Sometimes we can understand the obvious but miss an even more obvious point. If, say our jobs or 401Ks have become our gods, then what an insult it must be to pray to God to protect or bless our jobs or 401K (our gods) so as to increase our sense of security and thus cause us to embrace this other god even more. That is like a wife asking her husband for a hundred dollars so she can buy her boyfriend a gift. The Jews call this chutzpah, like you know the gall of such a person to ask such thing. Yet did we not have such chutzpah before in many of our prayers? That is the commandment - *thou shalt not have another god while in My Presence.* Before we begin praying to God to bless our jobs or 401Ks we need to stop and really consider just why we are asking Him to bless it. Before we begin praying for anything we need to consider if we are asking Him to bless or provide something that is more important to us than He is. Are we asking Him to spare something that we are depending upon more than God? Are we coming into His presence with *another God?*

Sometimes our god can be a good friend. There is nothing wrong with having a good friend. God delights in our friendships, he encourages them. But when that friend becomes someone we depend upon for something that God himself longs to provide that friend can become a god. How would a wife feel if her husband went to another woman to share his heart? She would be heartbroken and grieved that she could not share her husband's pain. Nothing wrong with going to a friend to share your heartache but don't forget to let God in on the picture. How about asking your friend to pray with you as you share your heartache. It may be that God is using your friend to communicate His solution to you. Yet, He still wants to be a part of this sharing.

A husband does not have to commit outright adultery to be unfaithful. I have known many men who will sit around lusting after women, pouring over pornography, talking about women in lustful ways and then declaring righteously: "Well, at least I never cheated on my wife." You try and convince that little wife of that. She is aware of her husband's lustful thoughts, she is aware of his roving eye and it is breaking her heart just as much as outright adultery. That is why Jesus said in Matthew 5:28: "But I say unto you, that whosoever looketh on a woman to lust after her hath committed adultery with her already in his heart." If a man shares his heart with his wife, then she is going to know of his lustful thoughts. Thus, that marriage relationship will suffer as the husband will shut his heart off to his wife so she will not know what he has hidden in his heart. Because if she were to learn all of his lustful thoughts, it would destroy her just as much as if he committed an act of adultery.

So too with God, if we are going to share our hearts with Him, He will know every lustful thought we have for other gods. He will know if we desire other gods more than Him and it will wound His heart. It will break His heart just as much as it would break the heart of that little wife.

CHAPTER 7 – A GOOD KIND OF SELFISHNESS

Proverbs 16:4 "The LORD hath made all [things] for himself.

From the first reading of this passage, it would appear that God is a very selfish God. But then the word selfish tends to carry a negative connotation. There is a positive spin on selfishness. Does a man not purchase a gift for his wife for selfish reasons, because he longs to express his love for her and by purchasing that gift he feels good, happy and contented know he is going to make the woman he loves happy? Surely he does it to make himself feel good. So what is wrong with that? Not all selfishness is bad. There is a good kind of selfishness.

The word *made* in Proverbs 16:4 is curious in the Hebrew. It is not the usual word that you find that is rendered for *making* as in *producing or creating something* which would be *'anah*. This is the word *pa'al* which is *working for a reward or commission*. We would use the word *employment*. I remember when I was working in building construction and my foreman handed me my check and said, "Well, this is what it is all about." I thought, "Isn't it about building these houses, the feeling of accomplishment, the chance to use the muscles God gave me and to exercise my brain?" But when it came down to it, I would not be on the job site for one moment if I did not get that envelope at the end of the week. The bottom line was that if I was going to eat and keep a roof over my head, I had to work and it was this particular job that was meeting this need.

The word *things* is not in the text, it is simply God made all *lama'anehu* which literally means *for His answering*. Actually, the word *lama'anehu* is a word for producing *something*. It is your common Hebrew word for *making* or *working* which is *'anah*. Yet, when you trace this word to its Semitic root you find it has the idea of *an impartation*. It is like Jimmy Durante once said when he asked a friend, "Who are you working for nowadays?" His friend replied, "The same people: the wife and the kids!" The English translation does not go far enough by saying that the Lord has made all things for Himself. That is true. But the word *'anah* suggests even more. God is working, laboring for his own pleasure. But His pleasure is in being able to impart the blessings of his labor to us. Just as a man goes to work every day to provide for his family because he finds joy and pleasure in his family and all the fruits of his labor are passed on to his family so he can enjoy their love and draw pleasure from their pleasure. The wife works all day at whatever job she does for the same reason, to be a blessing to her husband and family.

I remember as a pastor I was asked by the children of an elderly woman to speak with their mother and try to convince her that it would be the best thing for her to sell her house and move into a retirement community. Her husband had passed away and she was alone in the house and it was really just too much for her to maintain. I felt this was a good idea as she would really be more comfortable in a retirement community. Yet, as I spoke with this woman, I began to change my thinking on this matter. This woman told me how her husband had built that house when they were first married. Throughout their marriage, he would continue to add and make improvements on the house all which were for the expressed purpose of pleasing her. The house, its additions, and improvements were all to meet her desires in the house and not his. Then she got up and walked to a wall and touched the wall and said, "Don't you see, every wall, every door, every window was built for me? Every wall, every door and every window is my husband saying to me "I love you." Every morning when we would get up my husband would say to me, "I love you." He is gone now but he has left me this house that he built for me and now every morning when I wake up in this house he is still saying to me, "I love you."

What I find Proverbs 16:4 telling me is that, yes God made everything for Himself. He made it for Himself so that he could feel the joy and pleasure of saying "I love you." His greatest joy and His greatest pleasure come in being able to say, "I love you." He longed for the chance to say "I love you." So he created us and breathed into us his very breath of life so that He could have someone to whom he would be able to say, "I love you." Every tree, every blade of grass, every little squirrel that runs up to you, looks at you and runs away, every bird on your porch that sings and dances is God saying to you "I love you." God built this world, all of His creation, to be our home for this short period of our betrothal to Him. During our betrothal period, we are living with God in His home in heaven. But like any good husband, during the period of betrothal as he is preparing the home for his bride, he keeps sending her little love notes and little gifts to not only please his beloved but to also satisfy the longings in His heart to tell her how much He loves her. It fulfills the selfish desire in Him to express His love and of course, His beloved would not deny Him any opportunity to express it.

In this world where we are not living in a completed marriage with Jesus, He has filled our world with His little gifts and messages of love. It is found in all His *pa'al works,* that He *'anah made to impart His love.* As we spend our years awaiting our Bridegroom to come and take us to His Father's house and consummate our marriage to Him, He has surrounded us with all the examples of His love, as He sends His birds to sing to us, His trees to wave to us in the winds, His rains to refresh us and His sun to strengthen us. Would we deny Him the joy of expressing His love to us? Sure it's selfish of God! But you know what? I like it that God is a bit selfish and gets a thrill out of expressing His love to me! More than that we grow more and more in love with Him just as that young woman grows more and more in love with her betrothed during her year of betrothal to the point that she just cannot stand being alone without him so that one night her beloved comes for her and takes her to her father's house and consummates their marriage.

So too as we live in this world during our betrothal period to God we grow more and more in love with Him and every day through His *pa'al* works of creation he tells us that He loves us. As He keeps telling us how much He loves us we reach the point that we just can't stand being alone anymore so that one night Jesus will come and take us to live in His Father's house. We will then be allowed to consummate our marriage with Him and spend eternity living in His heart.

People fear getting old. They mourn the loss of their youth. But as for me, every year that goes by I am falling more and more in love with my Betrothed. I am delighting more and more in his little gifts. I rejoice over every little squirrel that runs up to me and twitches his nose reminding me that I have a Betrothed who is preparing a place for me in His Father's house. Little birds will land by me and sing and dance reminding me to rejoice, that my time with Jesus is coming. Many times a person walking their dog will pass by and that dog will look up at me and I can hear him say: "He's coming, get ready." I tell him: "I have plenty of oil in my lamp and it is lit and I am ready." He wags his tail as his master pulls his chain to make him continue on their journey.

CHAPTER 8 - AND HE GAVE TO MOSES HIS BRIDE

Exodus 31:18: "And He gave unto Moses, *when he had made an end of communing with Him* upon Mount Sinai, two tables of testimony, and tables of stone, written with the finger of God."

I was reading this passage in the Midrash Rabbah and discovered something I had not even noticed when I read this in my Hebrew Bible. The words *when he had made an end of communing with Him* is just one word in Hebrew, *kekalotho*. The NIV says, *"When the Lord finished speaking to Moses."* This is identical to the rendering by the New Living Bible which is a paraphrase. We consider the NIV to be a translation and not a paraphrase, yet this rendering from *kekalotho* is just as much a paraphrase (translator's opinion) as it is with the Living Bible.

The Midrash Rabbah puts an entirely different spin on this word *kekalotho* which really puts it into its proper context. You see Moses has been with God now for almost a whole month, *speaking with God face to face as a man would speak with a friend* (Exodus 33:11). The word used for face is *pani* which is more than just face to face. God does not have a face, the word *pani* when used with God is a reference to His presence, His light, His entire being. Literally, the entire being of God was *el (unto)* Moses and the presence or entire being of Moses was unto God. Then it adds, *as a man would speak to a friend.* The word for *speak* is *dabar*. Translators simply render the word *dabar* and *amar* as *speak* and never really make a difference between the two words, but there is a significant difference. *Amar* is just simply speaking, sharing chit-chat, talking about the weather, how was your day, etc. It is every day normal speaking. *Dabar*, however, is the speaking like that of a husband to a wife, it is sharing one's heart with another.

One dynamic of a married couple is that they talk intimately with each other about matters that they would not discuss with anyone else on the face of this planet. They share secrets, hidden desires and knowledge about each other that they would not dare to share with anyone, even a close friend. In Act 2 Scene 1of Shakespeare's play, *Julius Caesar*, Portia realizes something is troubling her husband, Brutus, and he refuses to share this matter with her. Portia is greatly disturbed that he will not share these matters of his heart with her. She tells him in this scene:

I should not need, if you were gentle Brutus.
Within the bond of marriage, tell me, Brutus,
Is it accepted I should know no secrets
That appertain to you? Am I yourself
But, as it were, in sort or limitation,
To keep with you at meals, comfort your bed,
And talk to you sometimes? Dwell I but in the suburbs
Of your good pleasure? If it be no more,
Portia is Brutus' harlot, not his wife.

Portia is so disturbed that her husband will not share this intimate secret with her that she declares she is not his wife but his harlot. She even stabs herself in the thigh to show her grief over the fact that her husband will not share his heart with her. This was the one thing that distinguished her from any other woman, even those that Brutus may have been sleeping with. When Brutus refused to share his heart with his wife, Portia was devastated and even stabbed herself out of grief and later took poison and killed herself just because her husband would not share with her a secret that was disturbing him.

In ancient Rome, it was not usual for married men to sleep with other women. In Brutus's position, he would have had any number of mistresses that he slept with. These things were not done in secret, Portia most likely knew of these affairs and culturally she accepted them. She may have had a few lovers of her own on the side. Yet, she had something that these other women that her husband slept with did not have. It was not that she was better in bed, but that she held the secrets of her husband's heart. Today a woman may do harm to herself out of grief and heartbreak upon discovering her husband is having an affair, but generally if he keeps a few secrets from his wife she may just say: "At least he is not sleeping with someone else." In the ancient Roman culture, it was the opposite. A woman could accept the fact that her husband was sleeping around. But if her husband refused to share an intimate secret with her, that would break her heart as much as it would break the heart of a wife who found her husband was having an affair in our modern culture.

So now we come to the ancient Semitic culture. Look at Genesis 4:17: *"And Cain knew his wife; and she conceived."* Some modern translations will say that Cain made love with his wife, had relations with his wife, had marital relations with his wife, had sexual relations with his wife or was intimate with his wife. Translators are trying very hard to put this into a modern context for us to understand yet the word used in the Hebrew is *yada* which simply means *to know*. It is used throughout the Old Testament to reference a knowing or deep understanding. The majority of the time it is not used to express the idea of a sexual relationship. The ancient Semitic concept of sexual relationship was on the mental and emotional aspect and not the physical. It was judged not on performance but on the knowledge that one had of the person they were intimate with.

Today, from our movie and music industry to our pharmaceutical establishments, the emphasis is on the performance in bed, and actually knowing the person you are intimate with plays a secondary role. Whereas, in ancient Semitic culture the "knowing" part was the primary role.

Thus, it is very difficult for us to understand the intimate relationship we can have with God because we are so focused on our culture on the physical aspect of an intimate relationship. The intimacy between a man and woman was to reflect the intimacy between us and God, yet with the emphasis on the "knowing" aspect, not the physical aspect of intimacy.

So, we have Moses on the mountaintop with God and something is going on. He was not some guru in a lotus position contemplating his navel. He was directly interacting with God, sharing his heart with God as God would share His heart with Moses. They were sharing their hearts with each other as friends. The word *friend* interestingly is *ra'ah* which is rendered in other portions of Scripture as evil. However, *ra'ah* is an expression of a *consuming passion*. If a person has a consuming passion for drugs, alcohol or sex, that can be evil. If a person has a consuming passion for their mate, their children, or even God, that is not necessarily evil. The rendering of the English word *friend* for *ra'ah* in this context may not be your best word in today's English. Today we throw around that word *friend* like a worn out baseball. We go on Facebook and see how many *friends* we have. We become *friends* with someone on Facebook with just a click of the mouse and end that friendship just as easily. No, we cannot use the English word *friend* anymore for *ra'ah*. The word *friend* in English has changed so much over the last four hundred years since the King James Versions (KJV) was translated, hat we are now scrambling to find new words to fit the context of the void lost in the modern use of the word *friend*. Today we call someone bro, *best bud, or best friends forever (BFF).*

When Moses and God spoke to each other as *ra'ah's* they were not speaking as *friends* as we know *friends* today, but as a *beloved,* as one who was *their consuming passion,* as a *mother cooing to her baby* and the little baby giggling and smiling at her, as two lovers sitting on a beach watching the moon rising thinking of nothing but each other, sharing their passion. That is why the Bible says, *"And He gave unto Moses kekalotho (communing)".* You see the word *kekalotho* comes from the Semitic root word *kalah,* with a prepositional Kap as a prefix and a personal pronoun as a suffix which literally means *as His bride.* He did not give the Ten Commandments to Moses *when he (kekalotho) finished communing or speaking to him.* Come on, He gave the Ten Commandments to Moses *as His bride (kalah)!*

The word *commandments* is such an unfortunate word to use in English. It gives the impression of "do this, or else!" God did not betroth Moses then follow it up by giving him ten orders to follow any more than a man would give his new bride a list of orders if she were to be his wife like "cook my dinner", "wash my clothes", "keep my house", etc. God chose his words very carefully here to show us clearly what the Ten Commandments were all about. He did this by calling Moses *His bride.* Sure the word *kalah* also means *finished or complete.* Jewish literature clearly teaches that man is not *kalah (complete)* until he gets married then he is *kalah (complete).* The word *kalah* means both *complete* and *bride* because a *bride* makes a man *complete.* Just as our love for God makes God's love complete. Without someone voluntarily loving God in return, His love is incomplete.

On their wedding night, a bride will often ask her new husband what she can do to show how much she loves him. The new husband will then reveal his heart to his new bride and reveal some of his deep longings and desires. Perhaps he will tell her not to have any other husband but him. Maybe he will ask that she never uses his name in vain or in a derogatory manner. Perhaps he will ask her to have one day during the week that will be reserved for just themselves. He will definitely ask that she not commit adultery or bear false witness, that is, lie to him. Surely on their wedding night, both will form a covenant between themselves with a list of rules that they will follow, rules that will keep declaring their undying love for each other, not rules to keep each other in line. If you want to call them commandments then go ahead I prefer to call them gestures of love. Thus, God did not give Ten Commandments, but ten gestures that man could do to express his love to God.

That is why when Moses descended from the mountain God gave to Moses, *kekalotho, His bride* a list of things he could do to declare his undying love for God, things that were very precious to the heart of God. And, if you truly love Him you will follow this list very closely. We call them the Ten Commandments but they are really ten ways to express your love for God.

If you look at it from a Semitic standpoint you can say that Moses was God's bride and lover and it will not creep you out because you will understand that there is nothing sexual in this bond between God and man. This intimate love is *yada'* an intimate knowledge of each other and a willingness to share that deep knowledge.

CHAPTER 9 – BELOVED OF FRIEND

Hosea 3:1: "Then said the LORD unto me, 'Go yet, love a woman beloved of *her* friend, yet an adulteress, according to the love of the LORD toward the children of Israel, who look to other gods, and love flagons of wine'."

The words *"beloved of friend"* is a very curious statement, because wasn't Hosea commanded to love Gomer in Hosea 1:2? Actually in verse 1:2 he is told to *take* a woman of prostitutions. Now in verse 3:1 he is commanded to *love a woman beloved of her friend*. In those days people did not get married out of love, marriages were arranged, fathers would offer a dowry or money to a man to marry off a daughter and men often married more for money than out of love. The idea that a person would marry a woman out of love was radical, almost scandalous. That is why there was a year of betrothal so the couple could have time to fall in love. That is a little foreign in our thinking as our culture allows us to pick and choose and we seek someone with physical attractiveness, similar ideals, desires and other things which we think will make us compatible. In ancient Semitic culture, there was the belief in a soul mate and the matchmaker would use prophetic gifts to find your soul mate. And if you were soul mates you would be compatible and you would learn to love each other.

Still, it was not unheard of for people to break with the conventions at times and marry out of love. Thus, when it came time for Hosea to find a wife, God said to *take* a woman. The word *take* in Hebrew is *qach* from the root *laqach* which means to *take a wife*, but it is also used for *taking possession of something, or capturing something*. Hosea was not asked to *love* this woman. In Hosea 1:2 he was simply told to marry her. But now in 3:1 after she has prostituted herself, taken on many lovers,

Intimacy With God

Hosea is now commanded to *love* his wife.

Some translations say: *Show your love* or *love again*. Yet, that is not what it says in the Hebrew text. That is only a translator's paraphrase. Actually, the KJV is really the most literal, *"love a woman."* The word used here for *woman* is *'ishah* which is the same word used for *wife*. Translators use the English word *woman* because it is generally believed that Hosea divorced his wife and so she was no longer a wife. This is based upon verse 2:2 where Hosea says he is neither Gomer's husband nor is she his wife. Actually, in those days a man could have many wives according to the laws of man, but he really only had one woman that he would call his wife, which was the woman he loved. David had many legal wives, but only one was recognized in God's eyes as his actual wife, that was Bathsheba, it was from her bloodline that Jesus was born. She was not David's first wife, who was Micah, but she was the woman that was his beloved, the one he was truly intimate with. In Hosea 2:2 when he says that Gomer is no longer his wife he was not saying he divorced her, but, as explained in the last chapter he no longer shared the intimacies of his heart with her.

Let's take a further look at Shakespeare's play, *Julius Caesar* in Act 2 Scene 1 at a further exchange between Portia and Brutus:

Portia: *Is my place only on the outskirts of your happiness? If it's nothing more than that, then I'm your whore, not your wife.*

Brutus: *You are my true and honorable wife, as dear to me as are the ruddy drops that visit my sad heart.*

Portia: *If this is true, then should I know this secret?*

As explained in the last chapter, if a man would not share his heart with his wife, she would not consider herself a wife. Even in Shakespeare's day the distinction between a lover and a wife was made as a wife was more than just a lover but one who shared the secrets of a man's heart and he shared hers. So Hosea is still legally married to Gomer, but since he does not share the secrets of his heart with her, nor does she with him, he does not recognize the relationship as husband and wife.

Not only is Hosea commanded to *love* Gomer, but it is also declared that he is her one true friend: "beloved of her friend." The word *beloved* in Hebrew is *'ehevath* from the root word *'ahav* used as a Qal participle. As a participle, it would have the idea of a continuing love or everlasting love. More specifically *'ehevath*, in this context, represents a love from the very heart of God. The word has the suffix Taw at the end and would suggest a love of adoration. The word *friend* is *re'a* in Hebrew and the Masoretes gave it a curious pointing because it clearly displays a play on two root words *ra'ah* and *ravah*. *Ra'ah* expresses a consuming passion. Hosea not only loved Gomer he had a consuming passion for her. Yet, there is that subtle play on the word *ravah* which means to be hurt or wounded. Hence, *"beloved of friend"* actually means one you have loved and carried a consuming passion for, who has deeply hurt and betrayed that love. That is why God commanded Hosea to *love* Gomer in the first part of this verse. Hosea had every reason to hate and despise Gomer for her betrayal of his love and passion, yet he was to continue to love her.

So too, with God toward us. We have betrayed his love and passion for us. He has every reason to be angry with us, condemn us, punish us, and send us to hell for the hurt and pain we brought to His heart, yet He continues to love us and forgive us.

Like a rejected lover God's heart weeps because it has been deeply wounded by our betrayal of His love like Hosea experienced. Oh, yes maybe there is anger there just as a wife is angry over her husband's infidelity. But it is an anger born out of grief and it is so intermixed. Can we really call it anger? Should we not call it anguish and despair rather than anger? To say God is angry is frightening, to say He is anguishing or despairing over our infidelity is heartbreaking. From the book of Hosea, I do not see an angry God, one who was ready to punish us, divorce us, send us to hell for our betrayal, but only a God who weeps with a broken heart and continues to love us and longs to share his passion once again with us.

CHAPTER 10 – BRIBING GOD

Malachi 3:13-14: "Your words have been stout against me" saith the Lord. Yet you say: "What have we spoken against you." You have said: "It is vain to serve God and what profit is there that we have kept his ordinance? And that we have walked mournfully before the Lord of hosts?"

There is an old cartoon of a man in a horse-drawn wagon with the reins to the horse in one hand and a carrot attached to a stick in the other hand. When he dangles the carrot in front of the horse the horse wanting to get a bite of that tasty carrot will start walking toward it. In this way, the wagon driver will get the horse to move the wagon but the poor horse will keep walking toward the carrot not realizing that he will never reach the carrot, nor will he ever get to eat the carrot as it was never the intention of the driver to give the horse the carrot. The carrot is just a cruel deception to get the horse to do what he wants it to do.

The Lord said you have been stout against me. The word *stout* is *chazak* which comes from a Semitic root meaning *to be stubborn*. *To be stubborn* means you resist any help or any attempt to change your course of action. No amount of reasoning will alter your direction. After being so *stubborn* against the Lord we respond: "What have we spoken against you?" The word *spoken* is *devar*. These are words from the heart and in this context, these words would be very meaningful and powerful words. In other words: "What have we said that is so horrible?"

What we have said is that *it is vain to serve God* and questioned *what profit is there that we have kept your ordinances?* Why is this such a horrible thing to say to God? After all, is that not why we serve Him? Why do we go to church, pay our tithe, read Scripture and behave ourselves? We are seeking God's blessing, for if we don't do these things we will not be blessed. Yet when we do all these things, it seems we are not blessed anyways. In fact, it seems those who ignore God altogether are faring better than are we.

It is commonly taught among many Christians that if we pay our weekly tithe from our gross income, God will bless us with great financial blessing. Yet, how do we account for the bankruptcy court being filled with Christians who have paid their 10% plus in tithes faithfully? Western Christianity is littered with the dry sunbaked bones of Christians who have faithfully served God and kept His commandments and yet ended up turning against God because they were not adequately blessed (paid?) for all their efforts.

If we are not blessed, it is *vain* to serve God. The word *vain* is *shave* which means to *make a worthless noise*. "What *profit* is there to keep his ordinance?" The word *profit* is *basar* which is *to plunder, to gain at the expense of another*. If you, as a righteous person would be bidding for a job against an unrighteous person, would you not expect to get the job since you are a righteous person? If you don't get the job you throw up your hands and say: "So what did all this honesty get me anyways?" Basically, that is what is being said here - that by keeping the laws of God you should profit over those who don't keep his laws.

Let's bring this down to a level we can understand by using a natural human relationship that God gave us to understand a supernatural relationship which I have been referring to in this book as the betrothal or marriage relationship.

Let's say a husband has a great opportunity to go on a weekend hunting trip with his friends. He knows his wife has made other plans for them so he comes home with flowers and throws them on the kitchen table and says: "Ok, here's your flowers, now that I did that for you, you have to let me go on that hunting trip. The old boy may go on that hunting trip with those flowers stuck in his ears and mouth. Yet, is that not what we do when we go to church, pay our tithe and even share our faith? "Well God," we will say, "I have gone to church, paid my tithe and shared my faith, now you have to give me that brand new candy apple red Porsche." Then you wonder why you end up with a fifteen-year-old Ford Focus instead.

Look at Isaiah 1:11: "To what purpose [is] the multitude of your sacrifices unto me?" saith the LORD: "I am full of the burnt offerings of rams, and the fat of fed beasts; and I delight not in the blood of bullocks, or of lambs, or of he goats." That word full is saba which means to be weary of, sick of or in good modern English, "I've had my full." Basically, God is saying he is sick of all the sacrifices and burnt offerings. I mean is that not what He commanded Israel to do and if they did they would be blessed? What is happening here is that the people are giving their sacrifices to bribe God, to put Him under some obligation so He has to bless them.

I find many people go to church, worship God, pay their tithes and even serve in the church who are really just bribing God. They need something from God and so they do all the things that they think they need to do in order to win his favor. The crazy thing is, you already have His favor, no amount of good works will earn you any more favor than you already have.

Let's say this same man who wants to go on a hunting trip with his friends comes home with a bouquet of flowers, gives them to his wife and says: "Honey, been thinking about you all day, I love you so much and I just bought these flowers as the only way I can think of to tell you how much I love you." He then embraces his little wife, kisses her and you know what, she will let him go on that hunting trip without a moment's hesitation, except for one thing. What man in his right mind is going to waste a weekend hunting down innocent animals when he has a little snuggle bunny like that wife in his arms. If she responds with a kiss of her own, maybe a shed tear or two, that old boy is going to have some second thoughts about leaving this precious little thing alone for a weekend. I know, the stuff of fairy tales, Hollywood stuff. But you know what? We usually come to God when we have a problem. Then we come with a dozen roses of praise and worship waiting for the right moment to pop our request on God but all of a sudden He just fills us with His presence and love and somehow we walk away from our time of worship forgetting to make our request known. Ok, that can only happen in a perfect world, but God's personal world is a perfect world and when He invites you into His world suddenly all that matters is basking in the sunlight of His love.

Well, it is obvious what the prophet is saying in Malachi 3:13-14, this *great sin is to serve God and keep his commandments in order to get richly paid or blessed for doing so*. But soft, there is something more to it than that. If you are really searching for the heart of God you will realize that by saying and doing such a thing to God you are accusing God of deception, like the old boy dangling a carrot in front of the horse to get the horse to move, yet never intending to let the horse have the carrot. God is dangling all these promises of riches and blessings to get us to obey Him and live a good life, but He never intended to make good on those promises in the first place. Like the rich man who loses his wealth and then his wife leaves him because he is no longer rich and cannot buy the things for her that she wants. The old boy is shattered and heartbroken realizing his wife never loved him to begin with, she only married him for his money. Did you betroth yourself to God for His money?

This is why it is so horrible to say: "It is vain to serve God, what profit is there in keeping his laws?" As the betrothed of Christ we are nothing but Christian gold diggers if we marry God for the money. I recently read where a twenty-nine-year-old woman married an eighty-five-year-old man. The man was worth a billion dollars.

Of course, I am sure that had nothing to do with it. Right? What we are really saying is: "God, I will love you so long as you pay me, but if the paychecks ever stop coming in, then I will just find myself another god who knows how to take care of me."

Can we honestly say: "God, if you go broke tomorrow and you are no longer the great provider…" Could we, like Job, say we will still trust Him? Some of us may have to face that test just to be sure of why we love Him.

There is a scene in Fiddler on the Roof where Tevye is reflecting on the marriage of his daughter Tzeitel to Motel and sighs, "They are as poor as church mice, yet they are so happy they don't know how miserable they are." If we are truly the loving bride of Christ, then God does not need to dangle a carrot in front of us to get us moving. We do it simply because we love Him in sickness and health, for better or for worse, through richer or poorer and if He chooses to allow sickness, poverty and the worse to come into our lives, we will still be so happy we won't know just how miserable we are because we will be blinded by love. We won't have to bribe God to get our prayers answered. We will be so in love with Him we will come asking what is it we can do to bless His heart.

CHAPTER 11 – ARE WE THE BRIDE OR GROOM?

Isaiah 62:5: "For as a young man marries a virgin, so shall thy sons marry thee. And as the bridegroom rejoiceth over the bride, so shall thy God rejoice over thee."

What can be more plain and straightforward that God has given us the marriage relationship to picture our relationship with Him than Isaiah 62:5?

Look at this verse closely. It is an interesting poetic expression. In the first part of this verse in Isaiah, it appears that Israel is playing the role of a bridegroom rather than a bride if we consider the word *sons* as male. Then in the second part, he is addressing Israel as if they were to be a bride to God, as this second part of the verse declares that the ones he is addressing are now the bride to God in whom He rejoices.

The word *bridegroom* here is *katan* which is another word for *marriage*. This word for *katan marriage* has the idea of joining together in complete *truth and honesty*. When God as the *bridegroom* is married to us He is joined to us in *complete truth*. They that worship God must worship Him in Spirit and *in truth*." (John 4:24)

Ok, that is God's side of the deal, he is the bridegroom. But what are we as the *bride* or *kallah*? In its Semitic root, the word *kallah (bride)* has a double lamed which represents prayer with uplifted hands. This word is a picture of reaching up to your lover with an open empty heart asking him to fill your heart with his presence. The root word is a little strange because it means both a *filling or completion* and a *wasting away*. However, the sages chose this word to represent a *bride* because a *bride* is to fill her heart with the desires of her bridegroom while her own desires *waste away*.

I know this flies in the face of our modern thinking, but hey, I'm just the messenger. Yet, is that not the goal of our relationship with God, to be filled with the desires of God's heart so much that our own desires just waste away?

I was recently reading in Jewish literature a rather interesting thought. The sages teach that there are three types of prayer. There is the prayer of a child to a parent. That seems to fit the majority of us. "O God, I know I don't go to church as much as I should, I know I don't read the Bible as much as I should, I know I only pray when I am in trouble, and boy am I in trouble now, but if you answer this prayer I promise...."

The second type of prayer is as a wife to a husband. Now, much has been written about how we relate to God as His bride. I have heard many sermons about being the bride of Christ and how a wife wishes for her husband to accept the leadership role. In the same way, God has established a man to take a leadership role in the household so we as the bride of Christ seek our husband Jesus to take a leadership role in our lives.

As the bride of Christ, He is indeed wanting us as His bride to accept His leadership, to understand that whatever He does is because He loves us and it is done in our best interest. Even if we do not like His decisions, as a bride must be supportive of her husband's decisions we must be willing to abide by whatever decision God makes in answer to our prayers. Most of us understand this and we sincerely embrace it.

Yet, it is this third type of prayer that seems to have eluded Christians. This is for good reason as we do not like to think of God as being vulnerable in any way. He is, after all, perfect and complete in everything. Yet, He has chosen to make Himself vulnerable to those He loves and love Him in return. Just as He chose to make himself a human being and come to this earth to feel physical pain like we feel, discomfort like we feel in this natural world and the threat of bodily harm and death as we feel in this world. He made Himself vulnerable when He came as a human being to this earth and He also makes Himself vulnerable when He chooses to love us and share His heart with us.

You see there is another gift that comes with salvation. If we picture our salvation as a betrothal or wedding ceremony then we follow this motif into our relationship with Him. In a marriage relationship that is truly successful, the wife has given her heart to her husband. That is a secondary gift that we, in Christianity, do not often consider as, unfortunately, many husbands do not consider. When a woman gives her husband the gift of her hand in marriage she is offering another gift, a sacred gift, one that she can only give to one person, she is giving her husband the gift of her heart. Unless a man really understands and appreciates the true nature of this gift, he cannot hope to possess this gift very long. In a sense, we are now playing the role of a husband and God in the role of the wife. I know it sounds odd, but let's play this out.

A husband wants to protect and provide for his wife. Now how do we protect and provide for the Master of the Universe? Well, one thing is to protect the feelings of God just as a husband seeks to protect the feelings of his wife. Women tend to be more sensitive and emotional and it can be pretty easy to step on her feelings and wound her without realizing it. You know, as men we can be just a bunch of dumb oxen. We will tread over a woman's feelings and then scratch our heads wondering: "What's wrong with her?" So too, we can tread over the heart of God and wonder: "Why don't I feel His presence?" To pray to God as a husband to a wife we are seeking to understand the heart of God. Like a husband will spend a lifetime seeking to understand the heart of his wife so he will know how to care for his wife's heart. He will take his wife's heart in the palm of his hand, examine it, protect it, care for it and gently caress it. So too as we pray relating to God as our wife. We take the heart of God, understanding it, protecting it, caring for it and gently caressing it. I know that sounds a little weird in our cultural setting, but once you get used to the idea you grow comfortable with it. God gave us a marriage relationship to help us understand our relationship with Him. It cannot be just one sided looking to God as a bride to a bridegroom, there is another side of the coin to consider, our beloved God has a heart similar to the heart He breathed into us, both a man and woman. He just does not have the male traits of protection, provision, discipline etc., he also has the female traits of love, nurturing and caring.

So maybe it is time Christians move to the next level in their relationship with God. We move from a child to a parent, a wife to a husband and how about as a husband to a wife. As a husband, we protect the feelings of God. We get out there and share the love of God to a lost world not only because we do not want to see our fellow man die in sin, but also because we know when a person dies in their sin it breaks God's heart and if we love Him we want to protect His heart.

A man who truly loves his wife will not cheat on her with another woman, not because he fears she will hit him over the head with a frying pan, but because he knows if he does such a thing it will break his wife's heart and the last thing he wants to do in this world is break that little woman's heart.

We do not seek other gods because we fear God will send us to hell and punish us in some way. We reject the temptation of other gods because we know if we yield to that temptation it will break the heart of the God we love and that should be the last thing in this world that we would want to do.

CHAPTER 12 – BRINGING PLEASURE TO GOD

Psalms 90:16-17: "Let thy work appear unto thy servants and thy glory unto thy children. And let the beauty of the Lord our God be upon us: and establish thou the work of our hands upon us; yea, the work of our hands establish thou it."

When you are in love you just want to do whatever it takes to bring pleasure to your beloved. You will purchase a gift and never give a thought to the cost as you want your loved one to have the best. O'Henry in his short story *The Gift of the Magi* told of a young couple who were so much in love and yet so poor that they could not afford to purchase a Christmas present for their loving mate and companion. The young woman's prize possession was her long hair that she combed, brushed and lovingly cared for. The young man's prize possession was an heirloom watch that he treasured and protected. Each wanted to give their love a gift that would bring great pleasure to their hearts. So they secretly chose a gift that would bring benefit and beauty to that which was their lover's most prized possession. The young husband purchased a set of combs for his wife's long hair and the wife purchased a special watch chain for her husband's treasured watch. When they opened their gifts the wife quickly pulled the scarf from her head to try out her combs forgetting that she had her long hair cut and sold to obtain the money to purchase the watch chain. When the husband saw his watch chain he immediately reached for his watch only to remember he had pawned the watch to purchase his wife's gifts. They only laughed and embraced each other and then put away their gifts for such time where the wife's hair would again grow out and the husband would be able to redeem his watch. Yet, the joy of the gifts was not in the usefulness of the gifts but that it was purchased through the sacrifice of what was most dear to each person in order to bring pleasure to the one they loved.

Psalm 90 was written by Moses, who knew a few things about the glory of God and what would bring pleasure to God's heart. In *Exodus 33:13 Now therefore, I pray thee, if I have found grace in thy sight, shew me now thy way, that I may know thee, that I may find grace in thy sight: and consider that this nation [is] thy people.*

He had asked God to show him His way. Why did he ask to know the way of God? Was it for direction, help? The Bible says he wanted to know the way of God so that he could *know Him*. That word *know* is *yada'* an intimate knowing. He wanted to know the way or the heart of the God he loved so He would know what to do to bring pleasure to His heart. God did reveal his glory, well kind of. The Bible says God revealed his *chasad* to Moses, *His loving kindness* and not *His glory or kovod*. God gave Moses what he asked for, but it was just not what he expected. He expected to find something that brought him pleasure, but what he got was the expression of the pleasure he brought to God. Well, he did get pleasure from God, his pleasure came from seeing the pleasure he gave to this God that He was learning to love.

Here in Psalms 90, Moses is saying that God will reveal his *hadar* to his children. Some translations render *hadar* as *glory* but *hadar* is really *beauty, majesty, and splendor*. Now, this does get a little confusing as God is going to reveal his *works* to his servants. The word *works* is *pa'al* which is *activity, deeds, what you have done*. To the servants, he shows what He has done and will do for them, but unto His children, he shows his *hadar* or *beauty*.

In the next verse, Moses talks about the beauty of the Lord being upon us. Here the word *beauty* is *noam* which is a word for *pleasure*. This, like the other words, is in a cohortative form and thus should be rendered in the form of a *blessing*. May God do good works for his servants and may His splendor and majesty be upon their children and may the pleasure of God be upon us all.

The rest of verse 17 is a little difficult. *"And establish thou the work of our hands upon us: yea the work of hands establish thou it."* The word *establish* is *kun* which comes from a Semitic root that has a variety of applications. I feel the best application here is *success or prosperous*. Thus Moses is saying: "And make the work of our hands *prosperous or successful."*

Taking a very close look at the syntax of verse 17 it would appear this success or prosperity is related to the *beauty* or *pleasure* of God being upon us. In other words: *"May all our works be successful in bringing pleasure to God."* Both servants and children bring *pleasure* to God, but there is a difference between the two.

So God will do good deeds for his servants and his beauty will be revealed to their children so all that they do will bring *pleasure* to God. Probably for most of us we would like to be a *servant,* as we would much rather experience the *works* of God in our lives. I mean all we get by being a child of God is his *beauty*, like big deal.

Besides that, many of us are so caught up in life's many problems and cares we are sure not bringing much pleasure to God with our present attitude toward our situation. We tend to just sit around feeling sorry for ourselves and worrying about the future.

So we start crying out to God that we are his *servant* and it is about time He starts to do some of this good *work* in us like healing us, giving us a good job or blessing us financially. Once that is done then we can get down to the business of bringing Him some pleasure.

Yet, I wonder if God is not bringing us into the state of a child. The word for *servant* is *avad* which literally means *slave, or bondage.* Do we really allow ourselves to be in total bondage to God, to be a slave to God? Moses understood this word *avad,* he knew about slavery. He understood the slavery of God's people in Egypt. Your life, your existence, your next meal was all in the hands of the slave master. As a slave, you are totally dependent upon the master for everything. When the children of the Hebrew slaves left Egypt, they were free to experience the beauty and splendor of God. They had a new slave Master, one who fed them and took loving care of them. Only this new slave Master was beautiful and majestic. But they were so wrapped up in getting their basic needs from this new Master, just like from the old Egyptian masters that they did not bother to see His majesty. In fact, they told Moses, "You go in the cloud and find out what our new Master wants from us and report back to us." I imagine when Moses returned from the cloud he told the people: "Our Master is so beautiful, splendid and wonderful. You've got to see it, you've just got to see it!" But the people were not interested in their new Master's beauty, they were only concerned about their next meal.

We have been redeemed from our old slave master of sin. We have a new Master who is beautiful and splendid and wants to show us his *hadar* or His *beauty*, but we are too focused on our personal needs, desires and wants that we never take time to see His *hadar* or *beauty.* We would rather someone else go into that cloud and tell us what He is saying. Once we get our needs met, maybe then we will appreciate that cloud better.

A new bride will spend weeks, months preparing for her wedding. Dieting, going to the hairdresser, picking out the right dress, spending hours putting on her make up all to make herself beautiful for her groom on their wedding night. Then when her new husband brings her into their bridal room he stands back and adores her, tells her how beautiful she is, he admires her beauty and in doing so he brings her great pleasure because she is bringing pleasure to the man she loves.

Does not God like to show off his beauty and majesty to bring us pleasure? For in bringing us pleasure we are bringing pleasure to Him. Years ago there was a movie entitled *Chariots of Fire*. When I talk about this movie almost without exception people like to talk about their favorite scene in the movie. The main character, Eric Liddel is training for the 1926 Olympics as a runner. He is also preparing to be a missionary. His sister is objecting to his spending so much time running and training for the Olympics when he should be preparing for his real job as a missionary. He takes his sister up into the Scottish hills and there he tells her. "I am going to be a missionary but I have a lot of running to do first. God made me for a purpose, but He also made me fast and when I run, I feel His pleasure."

You know, maybe running is not quite accomplishing as much as being a missionary. But still, God made him a runner and when he used the gifts that God gave him to their fullest it brought pleasure to God which in return brought pleasure to Eric Liddel.

Most of us just pick up our Bibles and begin to read it when we need something, maybe comfort, some key to getting our prayers answered or maybe thinking that reading His Word will sort of brown nose God into doing us a favor or a *pa'al, a work* or *miracle*. Do we ever really go into the Word of God to seek His *hadar (His beauty)* rather than his *pa'al* or *His works*?

Can a man just hug his wife, tell her she is beautiful, wonderful and that he loves her without seeking her permission to go on a hunting trip or to even get anything at all for himself other than the sheer pleasure of having the opportunity of being able to say: "I love you", to just get that pleasure in seeing his wife's eyes light up, to see her glory, as Moses longed to see the glory of God? Moses wanted to see the pleasure that He was bringing to God just as that husband longs to see the pleasure he is bringing to his wife.

Do you not long, like Moses, to see the glory of God, which is to see the pleasure that you bring to God? One day you shall, we all shall. One day we will stand before Him and see Him light up in our presence showing all His joy and pleasure that He receives from us. Then just stop and ask yourself, "What can bring me more pleasure than to not only know I have brought my God pleasure but to be able to see it?" Oh, the joy a husband feels when he brings pleasure to his wife or the joy that wife feels when she brings pleasure to her husband, the joy of seeing that smile. Those eyes light up! That hug, that kiss are all just a foretaste of the joy we will feel when we stand before Him.

Truly no man can see God. That is we can't see all His glory or pleasure over us and live. That joy would be just too much for the frail human body to handle.

You know if I were to write on Facebook that God gave me a brand new candy apple red Porsche I would get a thousand likes and hundreds of 'praisealleuiahs'. But if I say, "I looked up in the sky tonight and I saw the beauty and majesty of God and I could feel His pleasure," I could count on one hand the number of likes I would get. But you know what, if I had my choice between a candy apple red Porsche or seeing and experiencing the beauty and majesty of God and feeling His pleasure, I'd grab the latter in a heartbeat.

CHAPTER 13 – CAPTIVE TO GOD'S HEART

Jeremiah 3:10: "And yet for all this her treacherous sister Judah hath not turned unto me with her whole heart, but feignedly, saith the Lord."

We have to realize that at the time of this prophecy, Judah was a very religious nation. They had the temple of God in Jerusalem where the people faithfully worshipped. The nation was prosperous. From all outward appearances, they were a Godly people, yet God said that they *had not turned to Him with their whole heart.*

How many couples have you known who seemed to have the perfect marriage, they seemed so loving to each other and so happy in their relationship and then one day you hear that the marriage is over? Your first thought, usually the correct thought, is that they sure knew how to put on a show.

Judah knew how to put on a show. From all outward appearances they were pious, religious people but within that betrothal or marriage relationship with God there was trouble brewing. They had not turned to Him with their whole heart. They had not shared their whole heart with God.

If a husband and wife cannot share their whole hearts with each other, then there is trouble brewing. For one thing, that relationship will grow cold and stale. Then there will be mistrust building as each tries to figure out what areas of the heart their mates are holding back on. Eventually, as with Judah, there will be a total collapse in that relationship.

Take a look at this phrase, *sister Judah hath not turned.* There is an amazing play on words here. Every English translation will translate the Hebrew word *shavah* as *return* or *turn back*. What the translators are doing is looking at the qamtes at the end of the word *shavah* and assume it is a feminine ending based upon the reference that Judah is referred to as a sister. This is, after all, good grammar and proper. Yet, this dusty old Christian professor cannot help but ask: "Why is God referring to Judah as a *sister* to Israel? I believe this is a hint that there is a much deeper understanding of our relationship with God tucked away in this verse.

Now remember, the original Hebrew text had no vowel pointings. This came about a few hundred years after Jesus when the Masoretes feared that oral tradition would get lost due to the fall of Jerusalem and the Jews being scattered throughout the world. They felt the need to preserve the spoken Hebrew language in some written form. So they added vowel pointings to the original Hebrew which had only up to that time had consonants. You have no way of knowing how to pronounce a word correctly without the vowels, so they added vowels to maintain a correct pronunciation. However, at the same time, you really narrowed down the playing field when it came to translation.

You see in the original text the word we translate as *return* is spelled Shin, Beth, Hei. Actually, the word for *return* is spelled Shin, Vav, Hei. Because we assume the qamtes (vowel pointing for *a*) to be a suffix we then assume that the triliteral root is Shin, Vav, Hei. As I said, this is all very proper and correct. But when we hold the Masoretic text up to be the inspired word of God, (which it is not) we start to limit ourselves. The inspired Word of God had no vowel pointings. Oral tradition gave the vowel pointings and there was some dispute over what the proper vowel pointings should be.

Ok, let's just say that the word really is Shin, Beth, Hei *(shabah)* as found in the original text. That word means *to be held captive* or *to be imprisoned*. Another root word that comes from this is *yasav* which means *to dwell*. There is also a third root word that comes from this and it is *shavuh* which means *to make yourself like another*.

When a man and woman join together in marriage they are giving each other their whole heart. What does that really mean to give someone your whole heart? What does it mean to give God your *whole heart?* I hear people pray: "God take my *whole heart*. That is the best I can give you, my whole heart." Yet, even while saying those words I sense they are feeling like they are still falling short. It might be because they really do not understand what they are saying. When we look at Jeremiah 3:10 many of us have to admit that we are like Judah. We are acting *treacherously* toward God. The word *treacherously* in Hebrew is *bagad* which in its Semitic root carries the idea of a *covering or wrapper*. We are only letting God have our wrapper, our outward appearance, and not what is inside of us, our fears, our pride, our fleshly concerns etc. As the passage tells us, we feel like we only *feignedly* give him our hearts. That word *feignedly* is *shakar* which means to *be deceptive*.

Intimacy With God

Judah really looked Godly on the outside. They gave their tithes, their sacrifices, and their praises. They kept the law, they attended worship services. On the outside, they appeared very holy. But they had only given God their top layer and they were faking the rest - just like that so-called perfect couple you knew. They did all the right things, they said all the right things, they behaved the right way, but between themselves, they were only sharing the top layer of their heart and were faking the rest.

Many of these *perfect couples* whose marriage imploded probably wanted to sincerely give their hearts to each other, they really did not want to fake it. The loving couple they displayed outwardly reflected what they were longing to have.

So too like most Christians, we sincerely want to give God our whole hearts, we don't want to fake it. But we just don't know what it means to give Him our *whole heart*. Does that mean to live in some kind of monastic life style, never enjoying life itself as you are too busy praying and studying the Word, afraid that even watching a half hour of TV will turn your heart away from God?

That is where I look at that many different plays on the word *shavah*. To give God our whole hearts means to be *taken captive by Him*, to be *His prisoner*. A prisoner's life is ordered. Many who spend years in prison have a real problem adjusting to freedom. They cannot make a decision on their own because decisions were always made for them. Another play on that word is *to dwell*. If God has our *whole heart*, He is dwelling in our heart, he *holds it captive*. The third play on words is that we seek to make *ourselves like Him*.

I find Western Christians spending too much time trying to win God's favor through all their good works, their tithes, their prayers, and even their Bible study (reading) rather than letting God take their heart captive. In my search for God's heart, I am discovering that the only way I can know His heart is to allow my heart to be held captive by His.

You see if you worry that watching a half hour of TV will turn your heart away from God, then you are like a person in prison worrying that he will accidentally walk out of prison. It won't happen, the only way out is to escape. If you have no desire to escape from the prison of God's heart, then I doubt you have to worry that by watching a half hour of television you will accidentally walk out of your confinement. You have the same chance of walking out as a prisoner has of walking out of prison. God is holding you captive. The only way out is to make a conscious decision to escape, to want that freedom.

A married couple who love each other wants to be held prisoner to each other. We often hear couples jokingly refer to the *old ball and chain*. You have a marriage contract and it is not easy to get out of it, so when things get rough, you decide to weather it. The only way out is to make a conscious decision that you are leaving and then just walking away and filing divorce papers. You must want out pretty bad to go that far and yet people do. So too, you are betrothed or married to God, He is not going to walk out on you. You are prisoners to each other. The only way to leave is that you personally must decide that you want out and you must make the conscious effort to leave. I personally find it very hard to believe that if you experience the love and passion of God that you will really want to get out of your faith. But, hey, some do and God being the gentleman He is will let you go. But you will break God's heart if you do, just as a husband with a wife who dearly loves him will break her heart if he walks out.

Therein lies the sin of Judah, they did not want to be held a prisoner in God's heart. If you truly, sincerely want to give God your whole heart, he will arrest you on the charges of wanting to be a prisoner *(shabah)* in His heart and will throw you in the prison of His own heart and make you a captive *(shabah)*. He won't let you escape if you don't want to. Since you want Him to have your whole heart, He has it, the problem is that, like Judah, we find times that we are actually trying to escape so we can watch some particular half hour of television that would be offensive to His heart. No we are not leaving our marriage to God, we are just stepping out for a little while. A husband may decide to leave his wife for only a few hours and go to a strip club. He is not leaving that marriage, but he is leaving behind a broken heart.

CHAPTER 14 – CLEAVE TO THE LORD

Genesis 2:24: "Therefore shall a man leave his father and his mother, and shall cleave unto his wife: and they shall be one flesh."

Deuteronomy 4:4: "But ye that did cleave unto the LORD your God [are] alive every one of you this day."

The context of Deuteronomy 4:4 is teaching us that when others died Israel did not because they cleaved unto the Lord. That is such a wonderful promise that if we just cleave to the Lord we will survive when others die.

I took a close look at this verse the other day after reading about the earthquake that took hundreds of lives. There were Christians who died in that earthquake. Did not Deuteronomy 4:4 apply to them? I read about how ISIS lined up a group of Christians and beheaded them for no other reason than the fact that they were *cleaving* to God and would not deny Him.

Actually, Deuteronomy 4:4 is not a promise at all, but a statement of fact. Moses is just repeating a bit of history, pointing out how the people of Israel survived situations which would have destroyed them but didn't because they *cleaved* unto the Lord. Because they kept His laws they did not suffer the diseases that the others did. Many of the laws had a practical side which the people did not understand. I mean why wash your hands before eating, or wash your eating utensils with hot water. They had no concept of disease-causing microbes. They just did these seemingly meaningless and foolish things in obedience to God. Following strict dietary laws kept them from diseases that the other nations faced. They practiced good hygiene because God told them to, not because they knew the science behind it as we do today. They practiced strict rules concerning sexual relationships which protected them from sexually transmitted diseases.

Yet, Moses does not specifically mention the keeping of the laws of God, this is just implied. What he does stress is the idea of *cleaving unto Jehovah*. Bible translators have a real problem with this passage. The preposition *unto* is not used here. If this were to be rendered as *clinging unto Jehovah* it would read in the Hebrew hadevakim *laYHWH*. But it does not say that in the Hebrew, rather it is *hadevakim baYHWH*. It is properly rendered as *clinging in Jehovah*. But of course you do not cling *in* or *on* something you cling *to* something so the translators just play with the ambiguity of the language and use the preposition *to* rather than *in*. The same applies to Genesis 2:4 where a man is to cling to his wife. The word to or unto *el* or simply the prefix Lamed for *to* or *unto* is not there. Instead, you have *beishetho in (on) his wife*.

The problem is not in the preposition but in our understanding of the word *cling* or *devekim*. You see, we really cannot find a decent English word to use for *devekim*. That word has to be explained rather than translated. The closest we can come is the word *cling, hold fast, be faithful, remain faithful, be loyal or adhere*. Indeed a man should be loyal, faithful and hold fast to his wife as well as to God. Yet, none of these words come close to properly giving us an understanding of *devekim*. It just can't be done with one English word, unfortunately, when translating the Bible you have to come up with one or maybe two words at the most because there just is not enough room to explain it. We have no one or two words in English for *devekim*. You do not *devekim to* the Lord but *in* the Lord. A man does not *devekim unto* his wife but *in* his wife. By using the word *devekim* Moses was giving a double meaning that is so often found in Scripture. One meaning that applies to that particular time and one that applies to us today. By *cleaving* to God the people of Israel remained *chiyiyim alive physically*. Yet *chiyiyim* also means to be *alive spiritually*. In Matthew 16:25, Mark 8:35 and Luke 9:24 Jesus is teaching that whoever wants to save his life will lose it but if you give up your life for His sake, you will save it. Those who lost their lives at the hand of ISIS by *clinging devekim in* God may have lost their physical lives, but their spiritual lives in Jesus Christ will remain forever and that they cannot lose. No man can take that away from them. So long as we *cling, devekim in* God, *dwell in the heart of God*, we will never lose our eternal lives. We may lose the physical life, but we all are going to lose that one day, some sooner than others, but yet all will lose their physical life one day. If we *cling* or *cleave* in the heart of God we will be *chiyiyim* alive forever in Jesus Christ. So too if a man would *devekim* in his wife, he will never lose her.

So what is this *devekim* that we cannot translate with one or two English words such that we can use the preposition *in*? To the Jews today *devekim* which comes from the root word *devek* which is an attachment to God, having God always in the mind. The Jewish concept of *devekut* refers to a deep, meditative state attained through prayer and Bible study. In Modern Hebrew *devek* is the word for *glue*. It is also a synonym in Modern Hebrew for dedication toward a particular goal. Yet in religious Judaism, it is attaching yourself to God in all areas of your life. In the state of *devekut* one hears the voice of God and receives direction from God. One lives in the presence of God and heart of God. It is unifying all aspects of your life, body, soul, and mind with that of the heart of God. When a man and woman marry they are attaching or unifying all aspects of their life. They are no longer able to act on their own. They will consult each in all major decisions. In a true love relationship, their partner will always be on their minds. Their welfare, their care will always rank right up with their devekim with God. That is how He designed it.

So how can you put all that into one word? How can you say that word using the preposition *in*? I can't. Some would call this mysticism. If mysticism is to be defined as the Jewish rabbis define it which is "seeking to unify your entire life with the heart of God, seeking to always remind yourself that you are in the presence of God and whatever you do you do as unto God", then I have to confess I am a mystic and I think many of you reading this right now would fit that definition of mysticism. Mysticism has just become a dirty word in Christian circles because it conjures up thoughts of a pointed hat with stars on it and a crystal ball. That is not what I am referring to here when I use the word mysticism. A Christian and Jewish mystic is simply one who seeks to walk closely with God, who seeks the heart of God, who speaks to God and God speaks to them.

A husband and wife will seek to walk closely with each other, seek each other's hearts and speak to each other. Are they mystical? They are only doing what God desires for us to do with Him.

Those Christians who were beheaded by ISIS were obviously in a state of *devekut* for just before the sword fell they all shouted a praise to Jesus. Through their *devekim* or *clinging* to the heart of God they just entered a new life, a higher form of life spiritually. Their physical life ended, but they continue to live.

Devekut is a discipline. The Jews wear a skull cap or kippah to remind themselves that they are always in the presence of God and whatever they do they do as unto God. As I am not Jewish I will not wear a kippah out of respect for my Jewish friends, but I do wear a baseball cap, even if I am preaching in a church. I wear it to serve as that reminder. For over six years I have been on a journey to discover the heart of God. I have recorded that journey in my books and I still continue that journey always seeking to practice *devekim* or *clinging* to God. I carry no illusions that it will save my physical life. Maybe it will, maybe it won't. But I do know it is preparing me for another life, an eternal life with the Jesus whom I have grown to love more and more as the years go by in seeking to *cling* to Him or seeking *devekut*. The more I seek His heart the more I understand what the Apostle Paul meant, "For me to live is Christ, to die is gain." Philippians 1:21.

As a husband and wife who really love each other will do everything together will always be thinking of the welfare of the other. And when that husband is alone and faces temptation his wife will always be on his min. That wedding ring will always be on his finger to remind him that he is not on his own, that there is someone who is an intimate part of his life who will be greatly affected by anything he does. He is commanded in Genesis 2:4 to cleave (devekut) in his wife just as we are commanded to cleave (devekut) in the Lord.

CHAPTER 15 - DELIGHTING IN GOD

Psalm 37:3-4 "Trust in the Lord and do good, dwell in the land and cherish faithfulness. So shalt thou delight thyself in the Lord; and He shall give you the desires of your heart."

Probably the most defining word in a marriage relationship is trust. A truly successful marriage is one where each partner has total complete confidence in their mate to not stab them in the back. Is it any wonder that the key word in our relationship with God is trust?

Take a look at Psalms 37:3-4. There is a curious expression in this verse: *"Dwell in the land..."* Does that not go without question? I mean we are not fish so we cannot dwell in the sea, we are not birds so we cannot dwell in the sky and we are not stars so we cannot dwell in space. Where else will we dwell? Dwell here is in a Qal imperative form. An imperative is a command, I mean that is one command we have no choice but to obey. If the writer meant a specific place he would have used the word *esach* instead he uses '*eres* which means the *world, the earth,* or *the ground.* Why state something so obvious? Poetry to be sure, but also this a hint that there is something deeper.

Let's back up and look at the first phrase in this passage: *Trust in the Lord.* There is our keyword *trust* which in the Hebrew is the word *betach* which is the same word used in Proverbs 3:5-6: *"Trust in the LORD with all thine heart; and lean not unto thine own understanding. In all thy ways acknowledge him, and he shall direct thy paths." Betach* means to *adhere* or to use a modern term to *weld yourself* to the Lord. "Do good..." the word for *good* is *tov* which means to be *in harmony* with God.

When a married couple trusts each other they are literally welded to each. Welding is an ancient art and the ancients were familiar with this art. When you weld two pieces of metal together, the metal is heated to the point where it melts and the metal from the two pieces melt into each other forming a bond so strong you will break any other portion of that metal before you break it at the weld. When a couple enters into a marriage relationship they will literally melt into each other forming a bond that will eventually be unbreakable so long as that trust is a true trust or as welders call it a true weld. Genesis 2:24: *"Therefore shall a man leave his father and his mother, and shall cleave unto his wife: and they shall be one flesh."* The two will become one flesh, is that not what a weld is - two pieces of metal melting into each other and becoming one piece?

So if we are commanded to trust in the Lord, are we not forming a similar bond with God, our hearts melting into his and becoming one heart? When two people share the same heart trust is only the natural result. All it takes is just one act of mistrust to mess up the whole relationship. If a husband deceives his wife just one time, lies to her just one time, it will take a long time to restore that trust, if it is even ever restored. The two no longer are one flesh if they do not have that complete and total trust in each other.

How many promises have we made to God that we broke? How many times have we shattered that trust in God, broke that bond and then wondered why God's presence is so distant? Like a marriage relationship, if a man breaks that trust with his wife even one time, she can forgive him, but that does not mean that trust is restored. He has to work to restore that trust. So too with God, we break that trust just one time, He will forgive us. But we need to really work to restore that bond of trust. Can God really trust you? You don't have to prove anything to God, you have to prove it to yourself.

Let's return to that phrase in 37:3-4: *we are to dwell in the earth.* As indicated, unless you are an astronaut, you pretty much have that command sewed up. However, the word *dwell* is not *yashav* which you would expect and means *to inhabit*, but it is the word *shacan* which means *to rest, be at peace with*. When you weld yourself to God and live in harmony with Him, you really don't feel like you are a part of this old world. You just don't feel at home. Just as when a man and woman get married they leave their parent's home and make their own home. They can visit their parents and may even spend the night, but it is no longer their home. When that couple welds themselves to each other and lives in harmony with each other they inhabit a new home where they can rest and be at peace. The Apostle Paul said, we are ambassadors in this world and an ambassador must live in peace in the country he serves. Jesus said: "My peace I give unto you, not as the world gives."

So how do we find peace in this world that is not our home? The answer is in

Intimacy With God

the word we render as *dwell* which is *shacan*. We find the word is spelled Shin which is used for joy *and peace*. The next letter is the Kap which is a *vessel that needs to be filled* and the last letter is a final Nun which shows us a revelation of the light (I call that light Jesus).

Next we are told to *cherish faithfulness*. The sages interpret this as *to remain loyal*. The word *cherish* is *re'eh* which literally means *to feed, to nurture, or to shepherd* and *take pleasure in*. We are to feed on, nurture, tend, care for and take pleasure in *faithfulness*. The word faithfulness comes from the root *amen* and we know what *amen* means which is to be in total agreement with God. It is a picture of a husband and wife who nurture their oneness and agreement both emotionally and physically so much so that they actually take pleasure in being faithful to each other.

When this is done then we will *delight ourselves in the Lord*. The word for *delight* here is *'anag*. It is in a Hithpael form which makes it *reflexive*. It means *to be delicate*, as well as to *take pleasure in*. This is a romantic word. As that husband takes pleasure in gently caressing his wife, speaking gentle, loving words to her and sharing an intimacy with her, an intimacy that no one else can share, an intimacy that is special only to her and no one else. From this, we can get a picture of what it means to delight ourselves in the Lord. It is that restful joy, security, love, tenderness - all the things that God longs to share with us. He has given man a mate, a woman to teach us and demonstrate to us the relationship that he longs to share with us and that we will share with him throughout eternity.

Is it any wonder why adultery is such an abomination to God, why it was a capital crime under Hebrew law, why the enemy wants to pervert the relationship between a man and woman? The earthly relationship between a man and woman was to reflect the sacred, special and unique love relationship that we have with God. A relationship that God wants only to share with us, you as an individual and no one else. When we seek other gods we pervert this relationship as one would when seeking other lovers. It also leaves that betrayed lover with a deeply broken heart. Have you ever considered the fact that when you seek other gods (relationships, money, and earthly pleasures) you are breaking God's heart?

Then we come to that final part of this passage when two lovers are intimate, gently caressing, speaking loving, passion filled words of complete loyalty to each other and oneness, whatever that beloved desires, his or her lover will grant it if it is within his or her ability. So too, will our heavenly husband/wife (yes, the Sages teach a feminine side to God), grant our every desire of our heart. But as a husband quickly learns that when he gives his wife his heart and the wife gives him her heart, whatever he desires is somehow the same thing his wife desires. In that moment the only thing that man or woman desires is whatever it will be that will bring them closer to each other. If you have given your heart totally to Him, in such a moment you will only desire those things that will bring you even closer to Him.

CHAPTER 16 – HE WILL TAKE US

Psalms 18:16: He sent from above, he took me, he drew me out of many waters."

Some translations, paraphrases actually, will render the word *shalach (sent)* as *reached down*. I like that poetic expression as it pictures us struggling in a raging sea and God reaching down from heaven and picking us up out of the raging seas. There is no doubt that this is implied in this passage, but it is not all that this verse is really saying. It is saying so much more and expressing something even more wonderful than just reaching down to rescue us.

The Aramaic form of the word *shalach* does mean to *reach out* and the particular form that is used here, if it were in Aramaic, would be a Peal form which would intensify the verb making it very definite. If you were struggling in a raging sea God would, without question, pull you out.

Yet this is in Hebrew and *shalach* is in a simple Qal imperfect form. The word *shalach* means to send away, or to detach oneself, or something from you. It is a word used for divorce. It has a basic idea of separating oneself from something with a specific purpose or mission. It is in an imperfect form which means *He will separate Himself from above*. There is almost a hidden Messianic message in this verse. We are struggling in a raging sea and God will one day separate Himself from heaven and come to earth to rescue us. He will leave that heavenly helicopter and jump right into the raging sea with us to rescue us.

But here is the beauty of this verse where we draw on that picture of a loving marriage between a man and woman to help us understand our relationship with

God. The verse further explains that He will not only *draw us* out of the waters, but He will *take us* and then He will *draw us* out of the many waters. The word for *take* in Hebrew is the word *laqak*. Sure the word means to *take* but it means much more than that; it means to take as a possession, to take something that is of extreme value to you or to others. It is the same word used when a Jewish man announces joyfully, "I have *taken (laqak)* myself a bride." In fact, the word *laqak* itself means to *take a wife*. The picture is not God just reaching down from heaven and grabbing hold of us and pulling us out of the raging sea, it is a picture of God leaping from that helicopter, jumping into the sea, putting his arms around us, protecting us while we are still in that sea and then grabbing hold of that cable and bringing us back into the helicopter or heaven with Him. Yet, He is pictured as more than just some brave Coast Guardsman rescuing us from a raging sea; He is a lover, rescuing His beloved from the dangerous waters.

Oh, but the next words are even more telling, it is the word for *drew me out*. The word *drew me out* in Hebrew is *yamesheni* which has two possible roots with an amazing play on words. It could be *mashah* which is the same root for the name *Moses* and means to draw out or deliver. If this were the root it would be in a Hiphil form and would suggest that God would do something that would cause us to be taken out or delivered from the raging sea. Again there is a very Messianic suggestion picturing his death on the cross and resurrection as this would be an act to cause us to be rescued. You could almost picture something more from the word *Mashah*. At first glance it looks like the word *Mashach* where we get the word Messiah except the last letter, the Chet is really a Hei it is *broken,* that is, there is a space in the upper left-hand corner of the Chet making it a Hei. The *Hei* is referred to by the ancient sages as the *broken letter*. Perhaps God is sending us a message that He will send his only begotten son to die on a cross to rescue us from the raging sea and that His motive is out of brokenness. He is suffering such a broken heart over our sinful situation, pictured as drowning is a raging sea, that He is going to separate Himself from His secure and safe heaven and come down personally to rescue us and in fact to give His very life to save us. Like that proverbial shining knight in white armor riding up on his white horse to rescue us and take us away to his palace where we will live happily ever after.

There is another possible root word for *yamesheni* which offers an intriguing play on words. That root word would be *mashash* which means to tenderly touch or feel. It is used for one who is carefully examining a wound. When Jesus jumps into that raging sea to rescue us, He will first carefully and tenderly touch us, feel us and examine us for any wounds that He will need to heal. Yes, He will examine our own wounds and heal them while ignoring all the wounds that He suffered on the cross.

CHAPTER 17 – FATHER

Psalms 103:13: "Like as a father pitieth [his] children, [so] the LORD pitieth them that fear him."

Some people are beginning to think that I am giving men a bad rap with my talk of women being a gateway, having a special knowledge of God and all that, so I figure that I had better give a chapter to sing the praises of the father and wave the flag for the old man. Check out Psalms 103:13: "Like a father pitieth his children."

It is a given that a father will have pity for his children. Yuck, do we really want our fathers to pity us? That word pity sounds a bit too condescending. It sounds like a father can feel sorry for his son and maybe just lower himself to help his child along. The word that is used in this text in the Hebrew for *pity* is *racham. Racham* is usually rendered as *tender mercies.* It is a *caring, sweet gentle love.* Pity, my foot! Translators want to make sure the father is not made out to be some mushy, tender-hearted soul. Why he must be strong, enduring, and brave and if we are to attribute any tenderness to him we will just call it pity or mercy. Even commentators will not admit that the Hebrew word that is used for pity is *racham,* a romantic word. They will just wax lyrical about the great and powerful male who can show a little pity once in a while, surely we would not attribute these feminine tendencies of nurturing, caring and loving to a man. I mean a man is a man and has to be man. I have studied this word *racham* inside and out and outside and in and all around and I cannot get over the fact that *racham* is an expression of tenderness, caring and gentleness. If all a man is supposed to do is pity his child, that gives the impression of a father who is standoffish, who does not hug his child or tell his child 'I love you'. "Icky poo! That is girl stuff!" Yet, if David is saying that a father *rachams* his child, then that is exactly what he does. He does hug his child, he does tell his child that he loves him, he does weep for his child and prays to God with tears in his eyes for his child. Come on translators! Man up! Show some courage and admit that *racham* means a father does more than pity or show compassion to his child. He loves his child and hugs his child. Show me where *racham* does not mean that.

Oh, but behold, the KJV does not tell the whole story. The word *racham* is used as an adjective for the word father. A loving passionate father will show love and passion to his child. Some people don't like it when I attribute feminine qualities to God as nurturing, caring etc. He is a Father by golly and Fathers are not measly, soft-spoken, tender-hearted. He is a man, a fighter, a warrior, who fearlessly defends his family. Thus, we see God as a fighter, a warrior who fearlessly defends us and we are terrified of him as a little child is terrified of a father that will beat him. But David saw his God as one who *rachams*, is tenderhearted, forgiving, caring and nurturing.

Frankly, I don't want a Father God who pities me or even shows compassion, I want a Father God who will hug me, who will wipe away my tears, who will weep with me and pick me up and carry me when I just can't go on. I want a God who is *racham*.

The word for father in Hebrew is *'av* which is spelled Aleph and Beth. The word 'av for father has a numerical value of three. The Aleph equals one and the Beth equals two, one plus two equals three. A mother is forty-one, *'im* spelled Aleph and Mem. The Aleph equals one and the Mem equals forty. Together they equal forty-four.

A father and mother are partners in the creation of an *adam, a human person*. The word *adam* is spelled Aleph = 1, Daleth = 4 and Mem = 40, the numerical value of a human person is 45. A father = 3 and a mother = 41 and produce a 44. Oops, we are one short. To the father and mother we must add one to create an *adam*; that one is the Aleph = God = 1. Deuteronomy 6:4 "Hear O Israel the Lord our God is 1." It takes a unity of spirit, mind and body to create an adam or a human person but it cannot be done without the One, without God.

A father is an *adam* but he is also an *'av* which equals 3. What do we know as three? Father, Son, and Holy Spirit. That father is to be the human, physical picture of the Godhead. Indeed, I have found many people who see God the Father as they saw their own earthly father. If their father was a loving, caring, forgiving, patient, and understanding *racham* as was in my case, then they, as I, see the Father God as a loving, caring forgiving, patient, and understanding *racham*. If a person had a father that yelled at them, beat them, was cold, standoffish, never said I love you to them, never hugged them, the odds are they will see God as a father that will beat them if they sin, be stand-offish, never say 'I love you', and never hug them.

I found that when I worked with troubled teenagers many years ago that I would get nowhere talking about God as a heavenly Father. To them, a Father was someone who got drunk, stole household money and beat their mother. Fathers take careful note. The God that your child will believe in is going to be modeled after you. And if you are not a father that your child will love and cherish, then the odds are they are not going to seek out God as their Heavenly Father and boy will you stand in judgment for that one day.

If you don't mind, just one more thing about the Hebrew word father, *av*. The Aleph is the One or God and the Beth is the letter that stands for the house or home. The father is the beginning of family life. His function is to introduce the oneness of God into his home. The word for father is *'av* which has a numerical value of 3. What do we know as three? The Father, Son, and Holy Spirit. It is the father's duty to live a life before His children as the Godhead expresses before us.

CHAPTER 18 – GIVING GOD A HUG

Deuteronomy 10:20: "You shall fear the Lord your God; you shall serve Him and cling to Him, and you shall swear by His name."

Since I began my Hebraic studies over forty years ago, I was always convinced that there were different roles that men and women play, but I never, ever believed that it meant that men were superior to women. From my start of the studies of Biblical languages in Bible College and then on into seminary I have always been troubled by the way our translators translated passages of Scripture that dealt with women and hinted that they were in some way inferior to men and they were therefore to hold inferior roles. It seems Bible translation always had a powerful male influence and after forty years I am convinced our modern English translations are slanted against women. I am not saying these are mistranslations, I am only saying that there are alternatives which rarely make it into an English translation.

I have been in churches where a woman in the pulpit would be unthinkable and never would a woman be allowed in a position of leadership over men. I have been in churches where single women were told they must consider the pastor their male head and surrogate husband and any decisions they made, down to purchasing a car, they had to clear with their male headship.

The fact that I believe such beliefs are cultural and not Biblical is, of course, my own belief and I will not condemn those who follow other beliefs. They have just as much right to their interpretation of the Bible as I do. What I do find disturbing is that these beliefs of the superiority of men and the domination they have over women carry over into their understanding of God.

Intimacy With God

What I am referring to is the extreme that male dominance is carried to such that it actually influences how we translate certain passages of Scripture. Again everyone has a right to translate Scripture as they feel right in their spirit. I only demand that we see the alternatives before blindly accepting a translation from people, mostly men, that we have never met nor are we even given the opportunity to review their credentials and their personal biases and prejudices.

What I am referring to is how words such as *sod (secrets), racham (tender gentle love), ahav (love), yara' (fear)* and *devekut (cling)* are rendered. If the male is seen as the macho, domineering, fearless warrior, who must not show any deep emotion or even cry lest he be considered less than male, then we find that we will translate emotionally charged words with the least amount of emotion when they are associated with God. We will translate *sod* not as *sharing the secrets of one's heart*, but as simply *confiding in someone*, much more masculine, would you not say? Oh my, we would never translate *racham* associated with a male God as *tenderness, caring, nurturing, and gentle love*. No, we would never associate such feminine characteristics with such a Father figure as God. We will say He shows *pity and compassion*. We would never translate *fearing God* as a *fear of breaking God's heart or wounding His heart*. Why He is the Mighty, All Powerful Male figure of a God who would not suffer a broken or wounded heart! No sir! And He is a just disciplinarian and you had better watch your step! For, look out when Daddy comes home he will not have the tender heart of your mother, you must be afraid of Him. Then, of course, we will never say that *devekut* means *giving God a hug*. My, my, why God is a man, a man's man, he does not need a hug! Only a lady God would demand a hug!

Jesus said clearly in Luke 20:34-36 that there is neither male nor female in heaven, and Paul endorses that belief in Galatians 3:28. The Shekinah Glory is in a Hebraic feminine form and the very name YHWH is in a Hebraic feminine form. If we insist on gender is should be female. However, God is neither male nor female, in my many years of studying Hebrew from a Jewish perspective I find he carries feminine qualities as well as masculine.

And come on, does a man not experience a broken heart? Does he not feel mercy and tenderness for his children? Does he not desire a mate that he can share the secrets of his heart with? And does not a man desire a hug? Our culture has bred such a machoism that it denies the very needs a male has. That has, thankfully, changed greatly over the last fifties years. Women are now serving in combat roles. Women are now serving in executive roles and that of CEO's who have leadership over men. The church, as usual, has been slow to catch up.

Ok, alright, keep your extreme roles if you so desire, it's a free country after all, but at least hear me out when I offer a secondary rendering to certain verses. And the one I am pointing to today is Deuteronomy 10:20 where we are commanded to *fear* God. Suppose we do the unthinkable and render that as we must *fear breaking God's heart or wounding His heart*. I have addressed this earlier in this book. We are told to *serve* God. The word in Hebrew for *serve* is *'aved*. The word *'aved* fits very nicely with a husband seeking to do the things which will bring his wife pleasure. He will bring her flowers, take her to dinner, spend time with her, whatever it is that she takes pleasure in, her husband will seek to *'aved (serve?)* to bring this about. I prefer to call it sacrificing one's own pleasure for the sake of the one you love. To *serve 'aved* God is the same as this husband, laying aside our own desires to pursue what is pleasing to God.

But now the command *to cling* to Him. We think of *cling* as hanging on tight lest you get swept away by some danger. The Jews see something a little different in *cling* or *devekut*. *Devekut* in Modern Hebrew is used for the word *glue*. *Devekut* is gluing yourself to God, adhering to Him. In a *Devekut* ancient Jews sought to disassociate themselves from all worldly and fleshly concerns and become one with God. This can occur during prayer or during the study of the Word of God. Sometimes it is just a call to silence. Rabbinic literature teaches that *Devekut* is a high and deep stage of spiritual development where the seeker attaches himself or herself to God and exchanges individuality for a profound partnership with God. The force behind a *Devekut* is the love of God and desire for intimacy or closeness with God.

I have another rendering for the word, it is *giving God a hug*. How do you hug God? Hebrews 11:1: "Now faith is the substance of things hoped for, the evidence of things not seen." For many many years, I have studied this word *hope* in the Aramaic. It is the word *savra*. I am not saying Paul wrote this in Aramaic, but his native tongue was Aramaic and I believe he had this word in mind. After many years of study, I believe *savra* means a positive imagination. Imagination sets us apart from the animal kingdom as we are the only creatures with an imagination. Faith is the substance of your positive imagination, something you cannot see. Believing in a God you cannot see.

You know for a marriage relationship to survive a husband needs to hug his wife and the wife needs to give her husband a hug. If we are betrothed to God should we not give Him a hug once in a while and receive a hug from Him? Call me strange, call me weird, but I believe God likes to get a hug now and then and I render Deuteronomy 10:20 as "You shall fear the Lord your God; you shall serve Him and *give Him a hug*. Since I have already declared my weirdness I will tell you more. This is how I give God a hug. I imagine, I picture in my mind, Jesus hugging me and I am hugging Him and sometimes I go to sleep and Jesus and I are hugging each other. Sometimes I can spend hours hugging Him. Creepy? Well, ok, but don't call the paramedics yet, I am harmless.

CHAPTER 19 – GOD LONGS TO SHARE HIS HEART

Psalms 23:2, 6: "He makes me lie down in green pastures…Surely goodness and mercy shall follow me all the days of my life and I shall dwell in the house of the Lord forever."

Practically every English translation will translate that last phrase as *I will dwell in the house of the Lord forever.* Yet, this is not the standard Hebrew word for *forever*. We are automatically assuming that the house of the Lord is referring to heaven where we will live forever. It was this verse that I was discussing with an orthodox rabbi who simply shook his head and said: "You Christians do not understand the heart of David."

It was then I realized why the word *le'orek* rather than *olam* is used in this passage. Both can mean forever, but *le'orek* simply means *a length* and is followed by *yomim* which means *days*. Thus it literally means a length of days. David really seems to be talking about the remaining days of his life on earth, not in heaven. We assume the house of the Lord means heaven and therefore David is speaking of the afterlife. But Heaven does not exist in time, there are no *yoms days* in heaven. David is talking about the here and now.

Before this David says that *goodness,* which is *tov or harmony with God*, and *mercy* will follow him all the days of his life. The word mercy is *chasad*. Jewish literature teaches that in a spiritual context this word *chasad (mercy)* pictures one being sheltered in the heart of God. The word *follow* is *radapa* which is used in a Piel form and means to be *pursued, chased or sought after*. In other words, God is chasing after us to be in harmony with Him and to shelter us in His heart. He is longing to share His heart with us as a wife is longing to share her heart with her husband and he with her. We don't have to beg and plead with Him to be sheltered in His heart, we just have to stop running away from Him in pursuit of our own ways and simply trust Him enough to share our hearts with Him. Of course, that is the problem, many people simply do not want to share their hearts with God or just can't.

I know a woman who is now divorced. She says that from the very beginning of her marriage there was really no love there. She was involved in a church where the pastor had to give her blessing for every marriage. This woman was an attractive woman and there were a number of men in the church who sought to marry her but the pastor did not give her blessing to any one of them. Finally, there was one man that the pastor would agree to. This woman said she got married because she was told by her pastor to get married. She admitted that she never really loved this man and merely performed her duties as a wife. She tried to share her heart with him but he would not share his with her and as a result the relationship never really developed a bond. Before long her husband became involved in drugs and alcohol and started to become abusive. Finally, they divorced. Although she still remains a very attractive woman, young enough to begin a new life with a new man, she admits that she just cannot share her heart with another man. She has put up a wall around her heart and if she cannot share her heart with another man, then she will never remarry.

I know another woman who had a very rough childhood, she grew up in a foster home and was abused by many different men. She longed for a close relationship with a man, but every relationship she entered into that would start out so promising would before long collapse, usually due to something on her part. Finally, after receiving some Christian counseling she began to understand that she was afraid of intimacy, she was afraid to give her heart away because it had been broken too many times. Without realizing it when she would enter a relationship with a man, if it started to become serious, she would do something to sabotage that relationship. Through her Christian counseling, she began to recognize how she was sabotaging her relationships because she was so fearful of becoming intimate and being hurt again.

I interviewed another woman for this book who related a similar story, only she admitted that she could never have a close relationship with God. She longed for that fellowship with God, to feel His presence, she prayed for it, she had others pray with her but she was never able to draw close to God until a Christian counselor helped her to see that her fear of intimacy stemmed from her childhood which was filled with sexual abuse and rape and actually carried over into her relationship with God. Without realizing it, she was actually sabotaging her relationship with God and was fearful of entering an intimacy even with God. Thank God for Christian counselors who can help such people find their way to God! Yet, I cannot help but think how the enemy must love all the sexual perversions that we have in this world, all the rape and sexual abuse, the child sex slavery and all these things that damage the emotions of young developing minds such that they are even unable to maintain an intimacy with God. The enemy knows where to strike to get to the very root of one's ability to relate to God.

Let's look a little closer at Psalms 23:6 *"Surely goodness and mercy shall follow me all the days of my life."* That word for *follow* is *radapa (follow)* which has a numerical value of 284. The phrase: *for his mercies endure forever* also has a numerical value of 284. Ancient rabbis believed that these words, *his mercies endure forever,* opened a portal, as it did for Jehoshaphat when he went to war against the three kings. In other words, God is pursuing us with an open portal to His heart. Once we enter His heart we will find rest. You can bet the enemy is fighting tooth and nail to keep people from entering that portal, creating psychological scaring so that even though they long to pass through that portal into God's heart, their emotional wounds prevent them.

I believe hidden in Psalms 23, one of the most famous and favorite of all Psalms, is a key to opening a portal to God's heart of rest. It is in verse 2: *He makes me lie down in green pastures.* A *green pasture* in Hebrew is *dasha.* The spelling of this word reveals a built-in commentary, the word itself will tell us what these *green pastures* are. The word is spelled Daleth which is a portal to the Shin a resting place in the Aleph - God's heart. Note the word *lying down* is *rabats* which is in a Hiphal form. David is saying that God makes or causes him to find a resting place in His heart. God is the one who opens this portal, He is the one who causes you to lie down and find that rest that you so long to have.

When David says that *surely goodness and mercy will chase after me all my days,* it is almost as if he is admitting that he is running away from God. Just as so many who have been wounded by the enemy find themselves running away from God unintentionally. Yet, goodness and mercy will still chase after them. What happens when we let the lovingkindness of God catch up with us? He will then lead us to His green pastures. In other words, He will open a portal to His heart of rest.

Until the rabbi challenged me to understand the heart of David, I just assumed that when David referenced the *house* of Jehovah, he meant the temple where the presence of God dwelled or heaven. But the word *house* or *byith* in Hebrew has a broad range of meanings and could also mean the *heart* as a dwelling place. To fit the poetic flow of this Psalm it would be appropriate to render this as: *I will dwell in the heart of Jehovah for all my days.* To David, it was not enough to dwell in the presence of God, he wanted to dwell in the *heart* of God. These three women that I mentioned earlier all eventually found themselves resting in the heart of God. God chased after them until they were able to pass through that portal to His heart.

Dwelling in the *heart* of God and finding *rest* in the *heart* of God is really the message, I believe, of the twenty-third Psalm. When two people fall in love with each other, they will naturally share their hearts with each other. They will open themselves up and reveal the very depths of their longings and desires with their beloved. Yet, as these three women expressed, sharing your heart with someone is a very risky business. It makes you vulnerable to that person, it gives them the power to deeply hurt and wound you.

Thus we only open our hearts to that person that we can trust. We are so designed to long to share our hearts with someone that people will actually pay someone to open up their hearts to. They would pay a therapist or counselor knowing that that person is professionally sworn and legally bound to not betray the secrets of their heart. Such services have been very successful for many trying to find their way in their faith. Yet, the greatest fulfillment of love is when you can trust someone who is not bound by profession or law to protect your heart's secrets but is bound by love to never reveal the secrets of your heart. Some are lucky to find a mate that can fulfill that desire and many have found God to fill that need.

We know we can share our hearts with God, he poses no threat to us, and he is not going to go around blabbing to all the angels about the secrets of your heart. But this works two ways. If someone shares their heart with you because they love you and you love that person in return you will make yourself just as vulnerable by sharing the secrets of your heart with them. This creates a deep bond between you and the one you love. You both have made yourself vulnerable and it is this vulnerability that deepens this bond and also brings you rest and peace. It is that bond that causes you to find comfort in that person and makes you long to be with that person. When you find that you can share your heart with God and He with you then you are able to find rest in Him, knowing you have His complete trust and He has yours. Then you will begin to long to be with Him and spend time with Him which is what He is longing for Himself.

But remember it works two ways. If we can trust God enough to share our heart with Him, can He trust us enough to share His heart with us? Can He trust us to not seek other gods for comfort and security? Can he trust us enough to open His heart to us, to share His longings, desires, and pain with us? Can He find rest in us? For only when two hearts make themselves vulnerable to each other do they find that rest and security. Only when we share our hearts with God and He shares His heart with us do we lay down in those *green pastures*.

CHAPTER 20 – GOD WANTS TO GIVE YOU A KISS

"Numbers 12:8 "With him (Moses) I will speak mouth to mouth, manifestly and not in dark places and the similitude of the Lord does he behold."

Aaron and Miriam, Moses' brother and sister, began to have some doubts about Moses' leadership. Moses had married an Ethiopian woman and they began to question if Moses was fit for his leadership role because of this marriage. Miriam even suggested that God speaks to her and Aaron just as much as He does to Moses, so 'what makes Moses so special?' God stepped in and set the record straight.

God advised Aaron and Miriam that when he speaks through a prophet it is through dreams and visions, but with Moses, it is "*mouth to mouth*, manifestly and not in dark places and the similitude of the Lord does he behold."

The word used in the Hebrew for *mouth* is *Peh*. This happens to be the same root as the letter *Pei*. *Peh* means *mouth* or an *opening or entrance*. *Peh* is also cognate to the word *Poh*. This means *here* or *in this place*. Actually when you compare the use of the word *Poh* you find it is used to describe a very special place, a place *where things very important happen*. Note too, the phrase is *peh el peh 'adevar bo*. Literally, this is translated: *mouth to mouth in him*. The use of the preposition Beth or *in* gives us a little hint of something deeper. It indicates the touching of these mouths.

Other uses of the word *peh* is an *entranceway, opening, or border*. The mouth and the nostrils are the only entrances into the inner man. God went further to say he spoke plainly to Moses, not in *dark places*. The word in Hebrew for *dark places* is *chidoth* which is an *enigma* or *mystery*. He does speak to his prophets in visions and dreams, but these are often shrouded in mysteries and are not clear. With Moses he spoke *clearly* and *plainly*, there was no second-guessing. As dreams and visions are open to individual interpretation, what God had to say to Moses was plain enough, no interpretation was needed.

Then God adds a very interesting phrase: "The similitude of the Lord does he behold." *Similitude* in Hebrew is *temenu* which has the idea of *likeness*. Moses would take on the *likeness of God* in the conversation. This would be *a likeness in desires and wishes*. He could only accomplish this by knowing God's heart.

Here's the interesting thing of what God is telling Aaron and Miriam. God will speak to the prophet in dreams or visions. God gives a prophet a vision or a dream which the prophet will interpret. However, there is a difference in His relationship with Moses. With Moses, it is not God speaking to Him, but it is *mouth to mouth*, God and Moses speaking to *each other*. Then we have that preposition *in*, mouth *to mouth in him*. Taking *mouth* as an *entrance or opening*, it is coming out as a picture of God speaking to the heart of Moses by pressing his mouth against the mouth of Moses.

What Christian has not said, *"God spoke to my heart?"* That seems to carry more weight than God speaking in visions or mysteries. But soft, God is saying *mouth to mouth* or *heart to heart*. What puts this exchange on a higher level than a dream or vision is that it is not only *God speaking to the heart of Moses*, it is *Moses speaking to the heart of God*. You see, *mouth to mouth* is an ancient Semitic expression of the communication through a kiss. An expression of intimacy.

So too with God. God can reveal things to us in visions and dreams, but they are not always clear. He can reveal things in circumstances, coincidences, etc. We tend to guess that it is of God or God speaking, but we are never really that clear about it. However, if like Moses, we speak heart to heart with God and if we know God's heart, then what He speaks will be very plain and clear. In other words, if we allow God to *kiss us*, words need not be exchanged. I know that sort of creeps some of us out, especially if we are men. But remember God is of no gender. The Semitic people had no problem with men *kissing* each other without a sexual connotation like in our society, although they did not kiss on the lips, usually, it was the check or forehead. Still, they had no problem with *kissing God or God kissing them*, but we in the Western culture do. We cannot imagine such intimacy with God so we simply say God speaks to us *mouth to mouth* or *heart to heart*. That is a little less creepy.

A common question for many Christians, especially new Christians is how do you know that God is speaking to you? How do you hear God's voice? Moses gives us the answer, we will know God's voice when we know His heart. A woman will

Intimacy With God

not kiss her husband or boyfriend on the mouth unless she is sure he understands her heart. A kiss is a physical expression of the heart. In a kiss, one's heart does all the talking.

The ancients believed that Shepherds conversed with their sheep. Not in audible words, but with their hearts and the sheep knew their shepherd's heart which is why they responded. Perhaps that is what Jesus had in mind when he said in John 10:27, "My sheep hear my voice and I know them and they follow me." In the Aramaic, the word voice is *qala,* which could mean an inner voice or the voice of the heart and comes from a Semitic root word *QL* which means a key. The word *hear* in Aramaic is *shema* which is an *understanding*. The word *know* is *yida* which is an *intimate knowing*, it is a word often used to describe the intimacy between a man and woman. In a sense what Jesus was saying is, "My sheep understand my heart and as a result, I am intimate with them and they follow me." Jesus is saying He wants to communicate with us like God did with Moses, *mouth to mouth*, or *heart to heart*. A man and woman who deeply love each other sometimes do not need to even speak, they can just hold each other and look into each other's eyes and their hearts will speak more than words can speak. When a man and woman kiss each other they are not speaking with their mouths, but in that kiss, their hearts are speaking volumes to each other. So too when God holds us and we allow Him to kiss us mouth to mouth, we do not need to say a word, for our hearts are doing all the talking and we will naturally follow all of His heart's desires.

I remember reading about a very famous writer whose works were studied in major Universities throughout the world. Highly educated professors and learned individuals would discuss the works of this writer, debating his many symbolisms, metaphors and double meanings. Academics with advanced degrees, distinguished academic achievements would puzzle over many of this writer's complex nuances. Yet there was one expert on this writer that everyone listened to. When she spoke about this writer even the most distinguished scholars would listen to her. Yet she was a woman with just a high school education. But she was also the wife of this writer for fifty years.

There are many learned people out there who have studied the Bible and studied about God, but the real experts on the Word of God and God Himself are those who have *kissed* God.

CHAPTER 21 – WHEN HAROLD ABANDONED HIS DAISY

Deuteronomy 31:8 "And the LORD, he [it is] that doth go before thee; he will be with thee, he will not fail thee, neither forsake thee: fear not, neither be dismayed."

"Abused children will always protect the abuser, because it is all they know. They fear the person, hate the circumstances, but anything is better in their eyes than abandonment." – Kalav

Moses is encouraging Joshua in front of all the people of Israel as they begin their invasion of the Promised Land. He gives Joshua two assurances which give him courage and remove any fear. He promises that God will not fail him nor forsake him. That sounds like the same thing and a bit redundant. I mean if God will not fail us that means he has not forsaken us or abandoned us.

In Hebrew, there is a real distinction between failing someone and abandoning that person. The word for fail here in Hebrew is *raphah*. This is a word used when someone is pulling on a rope and his strength is beginning to fail. It is used for someone who is growing tired and weary of doing a task.

I remember as a pastor I would make frequent visits to a member of my church who was bedridden. Her name was Daisy and she lived with her husband Harold. Daisy was bedridden with rheumatoid arthritis. The arthritis had advanced to the point where she was unable to get out of bed. I always found Harold there caring for his Daisy, cooking meals for her, emptying her bedpan, bathing her, and holding her

INTIMACY WITH GOD

hand every opportunity he had. Harold never *failed* or *raphah* her. He never grew weary or tired of caring for his Daisy. One day Harold had a heart attack and was placed in a hospital. When I went to visit Harold in the hospital the first question he asked was about his Daisy and was she being taken care of. Then I just sat and listened to him as he talked about being in the hospital and failing his Daisy. He wept as his heart just broke over the fact that he was unable to care for his Daisy. Yes, Harold did fail his Daisy, not emotionally, not because he mentally grew tired of caring for her, but his body grew tired of caring for his Daisy. That is *raphah*, growing weary and tired of a task either mentally or physically. Sometimes you are just not physically up to the task, which is *raphah*.

But we know that God never grows weary or tired physically, but sometimes we think he will grow tired of putting up with us. But like Harold, his whole life was caring for his Daisy; she was his reason for living. Harold did not come out of that hospital but went to be with the Lord shortly after my visit. Daisy had no life-threatening illness and was given good care in a nursing home, yet she joined her Harold only a month later.

God will never give up on us emotionally or physically. We have the assurance he will not *raphah*. It is interesting that the word *raphah, failed* is in a Hiphal form. In other words, nothing will cause God to fail us, no lack of strength or desire. No matter how rotten and low down we are, even that will not cause him to give up on us.

While Harold was in the hospital I could not reassure him that he was not failing his Daisy, for in truth he was, but I could reassure him that he had not *abandoned* or *forsaken* his Daisy. There was a caregiver assigned to Daisy while Harold was in the hospital. Harold insisted that he speak almost hourly with that caregiver directing her on how to care for his Daisy. Harold did not *'azav* his Daisy. *'Azav* does mean to abandon and forsake, but it is not the cruel abandonment where you leave the person helpless, without any recourse. This is to *abandon*, by putting something or someone in the care of another. Although Harold did in a sense *abandon* his Daisy by going into the hospital, he did not *'azav* his Daisy. She may have been in the care of someone else, but he was still directing that care. Even though Harold was not physically able to be with his Daisy, his Daisy knew her Harold was still there, watching out for her. But when her Harold went to be with the Lord she was now *'azav, abandoned* and she lost her will to live.

Even if God should *raphah* or *fail* us, we could still manage somehow. But if he were to *'azav* or *abandon* us, I don't know about you but I could not handle it. As Kalav said, anything is better than *abandonment*. Being *abandoned* by God is more terrifying than His failure to heal me, or rescue me from a financial disaster. I can handle that. I'll endure a broken body, I will stand on the street with a tin cup, but

93

if God *abandoned* me, then all I have is despair.

So God promises not to *fail* us. That is good news. But He also promises to never *abandon* us. That is life-giving news.

CHAPTER 22 – SAMSON SPOKE HIS HEART

Judges 16:18: "And when Delilah saw that he had told her **all his heart** she sent and called for the lords of the Philistines, saying, come up at this once for he has shown me **all his heart**. Then the lords of the Philistines came up unto her and brought money in their hand."

I remember as a child, Samson was one of my superheroes, right up there with Jet Jackson, The Lone Ranger, and of course Superman. Yet, even at that early age, I detected a flaw in all my super-heroes, they were all such doofuses. I mean they would walk right into such obvious traps that even I, as a little seven-year-old, knew that these were ambushes set up by the bad guys. Yet they felt they were so invulnerable they would march right in, head high, get punched right in the jaw and would be out for the count. Old Samson was right there on top of the list. I mean, you would think that after pretending to tell Delilah the secret of his strength three times and each time he tells her she blabs it to the Philistines who come marching in to arrest him, he would begin to wake up. You think after three times of betrayal it would finally dawn on him that this old gal is trying to scam him. Fool me once shame on you, fool me twice, well shame on old Samson.

Come on, let's face it, Samson was no dumb jock who just fell off the turnip truck. Three times he told Delilah the secret to his strength, and each time he told her the truth. The bow strings that she tied him up with were in the Hebrew *yatarim*. We would call this today *cat gut* - something off a dead animal. Such material was used in those days to make the strings for their bows. Of course, as a Nazarite,

Samson could not touch a dead animal, so bingo, he should have lost his strength right then and there, but he didn't. That is quite interesting that he did not lose his strength and I am sure Samson was intrigued by this as well. So why not spill his guts (pun intended) to win a one night stand with a knock out like Delilah? So when she puts on the betrayed innocent-girl-next-door act again he decides to drop another card and tells her to tie him up with *avar kadeshim* which many translations call *new ropes*. Actually *avar* refers to an entangling type vine and *kadeshim* means *fresh or alive*. This Hebrew word is typically used to describe a *grapevine*. As a Nazarite Samson could not drink or even touch wine. Once again he discovered he did not lose his strength. This was a new revelation for him. I am sure he was thinking about all those years of growing up in fundamentalism with all his 'no drinking, no smoking nor going out with girls that do' when all along he could have been partying on.

Well old Delilah was not impressed and her employers were getting pretty impatient with her, so she really put on the nag. This third time she was to interweave the seven locks of his hair. Within the Nazarite vow, the seven locks represented a divine act and a commitment to a divine call. To interweave the seven locks would symbolically be breaking his Nazarite vow. Yet, still he did not lose his strength.

The fourth time was when he blew it. It was not the cutting off of his seven locks that caused him to lose his strength; he already blew that hair part with the interweaving of his locks. It had to be something else. Something that is so obvious like what millions of viewers see when they watch the Bachelor and Bachelorette series that continues to make the show a success. Everyone knows these little trysts and romantic expletives are a sham. I mean the whole thing is a game, after all. Each contestant is trying to win. Let's face it; they are cast for this role because they can really put on the dog yet deep inside everyone wants to believe and fantasize that these bachelors or bachelorettes are really in love. However, when the lights come on we all know better. Still, everyone is waiting for that knight in shining armor who will show them one thing. The audience is waiting and hoping to hear or *see* one thing. They are waiting to *see* one contestant speak his or her *heart*. Then, you know, like everything starts to get misty and all the old timers sigh and say: "How sweet."

We all have seen the *dude, Christian*. You know, the one who has all the right words, appears happy, spiritual, spouting out praisealleuiahs faster than a sailor spews out profanities. You know it is all phony; it is all an act just to manipulate you into voting for him as the spiritual top dog in the church. He is vying for some key position on the worship team or on the platform. But to win your vote he has to appear so holy that the Vatican could hire him to model for a holy card. But it is the ones who *speak their hearts* that you know are the genuine article. It is the preacher who lives every sermon he preaches that wins the respect of his congregation and

Intimacy With God

not the one preaching the newest fads and spiritual catch words like turn to your neighbor and say, "be blessed." I mean if it worked for the TV preachers it should work for the fifty people congregation of the Eighth Baptist Church in Cornersville.

Three times Samson shared his secrets with Delilah, three times she called the Philistines, and three times they came and had to run for their lives without giving Delilah a drachma. Yet, this fourth time they came, not only trusting that Delilah had the secret but also so convinced that she had the secret, that they brought her money. Now, why would they suddenly believe her after being fooled three times?

The answer is in the words: *He has shown me all his heart.* It was something that was very different this time, it was not Sampson's hair-brained sounding story of being a Nazarite. Delilah probably knew about as much of a Nazarite as we do. But it was something else. Note in verse 19 that Samson did not lose his strength when Delilah cut off his seven locks, he lost it when she *afflicted* him. The word *afflict* comes from the root word *'anah* which has a wide range of meanings. But in its Semitic origins, it has the idea of someone exercising control over someone else. Within the Canaanite language, the root form of this word has a sexual connotation. Yeah, that was some *affliction*. Might I be so afflicted! This word is in a Piel form so Delilah was not only exercising control over Sampson physically but emotionally as well. The other times when she tried to *afflict* or *anah* him, it didn't work, he was holding back, he still had his strength. This time, however, he lost his strength. The reason is, is because he *gave her his heart*, she had him not only physically, emotionally, but now she had him spiritually. What belonged only to God as a Nazarite, Samson took from God and gave it to Delilah. The bottom line is that Samson said to God: "I love her more than I love you." It broke God's heart and like a broken-hearted lover, and the gentleman that God is, he removed Himself from Samson and the rest is history.

I have studied Classical Hebrew for over forty years and I have always pondered what the word *heart* or *lev* in Hebrew really means. I cannot give it words, because, like Delilah, you have to *see* it or *ra'ah* it. *Ra'ah* is not only seeing with physical eyes, but with *spiritual eyes* as well. Poets may write hundreds of verses to describe it, but you only know it if you *see it*.

Many Christians are like the young woman candidate on the Bachelor series. When she is alone with each bachelor, she tells him how much she loves him, how she longs to be with him, how wonderful he is. Yet she is saying the same things to each bachelor, and is not really speaking her heart to any, at least not in the Biblical sense. We come to church on Sunday, tell God how we love Him, how wonderful He is, how we long to be with Him, and then walk outside the church and express the same love for the latest professional ball team, our job, hobby or bank account. But somewhere we have to make a choice as to who gets the rose. Somewhere we are going to *speak our heart*, give our hearts to just one of these (G)god(s) in our lives. Are we going to speak our hearts and give our hearts to God Jehovah, or to a Delilah?

CHAPTER 23 – A TRYSTING PLACE

Exodus 40:35: "And Moses could not enter the Tent of Meeting, for the cloud rested (shakhan) upon it, and the glory of the Lord filled the Tabernacle."

Maybe I am just an old romantic, but I love those gothic romance novels. My favorite author was Grace Livingston Hill who was a master of good old-fashioned romance. You know, the poor struggling beautiful young girl who has many suitors that would marry her and take care of her but finally that one noble, handsome Donald Trump style rich comes along and carries her off to their trysting place? A trysting place is an old-fashioned word where a young couple in love can go to meet in private and be alone together. A husband and wife have their little private place that they can go to, where no one else is around and it is there that they can be intimate. They can do things and say things to each other that they cannot do or say in public. It is a time when they can just unburden their soul and share their hearts deepest longings for each other. Actually, without a trysting place, a romantic relationship would quickly die. So too we need that private place to go to every day: a garden, a special room, a warehouse… where the Shekinah can manifest itself and we can share an intimacy with our creator so that relationship will never die. I believe there is a word in Hebrew that would properly translate as a trysting place, it is the word shahkan where the Shekinah can *aniemi (tightly embrace)* us.

Moses could not enter the Tent of Meeting because of the *Shekinah glory*. The Talmud and other Jewish literature are filled with references to the *Shekinah glory*. Christians hate the word *mystical* and yet the word *Shekinah* that Christians love to use is a mystical word. It is simply referring to the presence of God. The word, *Shekinah* itself is not found in the Biblical text. This word is really an extra-biblical word that mystical Jewish rabbis coined. They took the word *shakhan* which unromantically means a *dwelling place* and put it into a hiphil form so it literally means *he is caused to dwell.* Then they added a feminine ending. In Mishnaic Hebrew the word is often referred to as birds *nesting.* (Talmud Baba Kammah 92b). Ever wonder why we talk about the *birds and the bees?* Perhaps it has its origins in the word *shakhan* and gives my rendering of *shakhan* as a *trysting place* a little creditability. I can't help but feel many of our Bible translators are just dusty old professors sitting up in their ivy towered offices who haven't kissed their wives in twenty years. I bet you any number of my youthful, red-blooded American students would have jumped at the chance to translate *shakhan* as a *trysting place.*

The word *shakhan* has also been used to express the idea of royalty *or royal residence.* Sigh! What is a better way to describe this sacred, secret place where young couples meet to express their undying love for each other than a royal residence where every young woman is made to feel like a princess and every young man like a dashing young prince? The Greek word *skene - dwelling* is thought to be derived from *shakhan.* The word *Tabernacle (mishcan)* is a derivative of the same root and it is also used in the sense of a *dwelling-place.* In classic Jewish thought the *Shekinah* refers to dwelling or settling in a special place so that while in proximity to the *Shekinah*, the connection to God is more readily perceivable. Tell me that does not describe a trysting place where the connection between two lovers is readily more perceivable. The word *shakhan* is different than the other Hebrew word for dwelling which is *yashav* in that *shakhan* is more direct and means to take up residence in one place for an extended period of time.

It is in the *Shekinah Glory* that we find our trysting place with God. Where does the *Shekinah* manifest itself? It is the Temple and Tabernacle that is most prevalent in Jewish literature. However, the Talmud reports that it may be found in acts of public prayer. "Where ten are gathered for prayer, there the Shekinah rest." Talmud Sanhedrin 39a. It is also found in righteous judgment: "When three sit as judges, the *Shekinah* is with them." Talmud Berachot 6a. Jesus may have been referencing this when he said: "Where two or three are gathered together, there am I in the midst." Maybe this is a reference to prayer, maybe to Bible study, I am not sure, but what I am sure of is it is one big love feast with Jesus as all come into unity with Him. The *Shekinah* is also found when in personal need - Talmud Shabbat 12b. It was also manifested when the prophets prophesied. II Kings 3:15: "And now, bring for me a musician, and it happened that when the music played, God's hand rested upon him (Elisha)." Elisha then received his prophecy.

Yet, is not God omnipresent? How can he dwell in one location? This is where we miss it. The rabbinic teaching is that the omnipresence of God is Heavenly, it is his masculine nature, the part that protects, provides, watches over. However, the

Shekinah is the earthly, the feminine nature where He nurtures, comforts, shares intimately with you.

Josephus in Antiquities 14.7.1 gives an account of Herod raiding the tomb of David and Solomon to acquire its wealth to finance the rebuilding of the temple. Josephus records that as two guards entered the tomb they were *slain by a flame* of the *Shekinah* glory. It shook old Herod up so much he sealed off the tomb never to re-enter.

Eusebius (church historian and scholar 260-340 CE records that the *Shekinah* glory was seen leaving the temple in 66 AD and alighting on the Mount of Olives. Josephus and a witness named Rabbi Jonathan also records the same account. This is really why the Mt of Olives has traditionally been such a special place for Christians. Yet do we need to travel to the Mt of Olives to experience the *Shekinah* glory?

John says: "In the beginning was the Word (logos) and the Word was with God and the Word was God. All things were made by Him and without Him was not anything made that was made." John 1:1-2.

The King James Version of 1611 and all versions that have stemmed from it, have attached the Masculine gender to the Greek concept of the *Logos*. The eight prior English translations give *logos* a neuter gender: "By it all things were made." This is important, which is why we must catch this. Jesus is the *Logos* which is why later translations give it a masculine gender. However, Jewish teaching tells us that it was the *Shekinah* glory that created the world. Prior to His appearance on Earth, Jesus was the *Shekinah* glory and when the physical manifestation ascended to heaven his earthly manifestation as the *Shekinah* glory remained. Paul tells us that He will *"never leave us…"* Hebrews 13:5. The word *leave* in the Greek is *aniemi* which means to *tightly embrace*. He cannot do that from heaven. So, although his physical body ascended to heaven, His earthly presence, the *Shekinah* glory, the feminine nature of nurturing, comforting etc. remains to *aniemi, tightly embrace u*s.

As Christians we have the very living, loving life of Jesus Christ inside of us, we are now the temple of God which means that the *Shekinah* glory rests within us. When we allow the light of Jesus Christ to shine out of us, people will see the presence of God. You think that little bird or squirrel is attracted to you because of you? Perhaps they sense that living, loving life of Jesus Christ in you and it is the *Shekinah* glory they are attracted to.

But soft, remember the Shekinah means *a dwelling place*. Paul makes it clear that this is our earthly bodies: "We have this treasure in earthly bodies…" II Cor. 4:7. How about that? The Shekinah glory now dwells within us.

Yet there is more, the Shekinah glory also demands *a physical location*. As Jesus went to the garden, and Paul to the desert, we too need a place to go: A place far from the restless places, a place that is protected by trees and flowers. It is a place where no one else is around and His Shekinah glory can manifest itself to soothe our troubled minds. It is a trysting place where we can rest in the arms of God as He speaks softly and lovingly to us and we share the love of our hearts with Him. Find it, find someplace and take Jesus there and declare that it is now your *trysting place*.

CHAPTER 24 – KNOWING GOD'S THOUGHTS

Isaiah 55:8: "For my thoughts are not your thoughts, neither are your ways my ways, saith the Lord."

My parents were married for 67 years. I used to listen in amazement as they spoke to each other. "You think we should visit…" "Yes, I would love to see them, how about…" "This evening would be fine." They had spent so much time together and grew together in such intimacy, that they could anticipate what the other was thinking. So too in knowing the thoughts of God. The more time you spend with Him, the more intimate you become, the more you can anticipate His thoughts

The word for *thought* in Isaiah 55:8 is not *sh'ar* as it is in Proverbs 23:7. Here the word is *chashav. Sh'ar* has the idea of thinking to make a decision; this thinking is to *invent or create* or *to lay out a plan*. In the context of Isaiah 55:8 it would be to *lay out directions*. Hence your directions or maps are not God's maps. Your ways are not God's ways. The word way is *derek. Derek* has the idea of following a path that leads to God's purpose.

This is clearly Hebrew poetry using the discipline of parallelism. I once knew a guy who had a Ph.D. in Poetry. The University where he taught had published a book of his poetry. Some would read his poetry and question whether it was really poetry as some of his poems did not rhyme or have a certain meter. But to say that because a particular work was not poetry because it did not rhyme would be like saying a painting of a house is not art because it does not look like a house. This poet told me that rhyme and meter were disciplines of poetry, but not poetry itself. The poetry laid in his choice of words, the hidden meanings, the metaphors and similes and the ability of his words to say many things to many people.

Hebrew poetry is just like poetry in English except it has different disciplines. Poetry is still embedded with hidden and mysterious meanings and interpretations. Poetry is universal in its ability to paint a picture with words.

In this verse, we have a picture of a person taking a journey. This could be a journey of life; it could be a journey in a relationship, a journey in a job, or a journey in a ministry, or even a sermon. When you take a journey you start out with directions. When I check my GPS I find I have certain options. I can choose directions that will involve the use of the Toll Road or highways. I can take the shortest route or the longest route. There are a number of roads that will lead me to my destination. This is the picture painted with poetic words here. There are various options to reach God's purpose, there are various roads that lead to God's purpose.

I drive a bus for the disabled. Yesterday I had to drive to La Grange for a pickup. When I received the call I was at least a half hour to forty-five minutes away. I needed to pick the route that would get me there the quickest, so I chose the quickest route. However, the quickest route took me past a school just letting out and then railroad tracks where I had to wait for a long freight train to pass. The shortest route, the route I thought best ended up taking me longer to reach my destination than had I chosen the longer route. I took the way which seemed right unto me but the end thereof was a way which made me late for my next pick up.

Proverbs 14:12: "There is a way which seems right unto a man, but the end thereof are the ways of death." Again we have the word *derek* for *ways*. As *derek* represents a *path* to God, the *derek* of *death* would be a way of *spiritual death*.

History is littered with the dry, sun-baked bones of Christians who convinced themselves that their thoughts were God's thoughts and ended on a path that was not God's path. Many times we reach God's purpose but because we chose the path which seemed right unto us and was not God's path we ended up going over some very rough road. Many end up getting discouraged before reaching God's purpose and just give up and end up *spiritually dead*.

We often say that God is testing us, or putting us through trials to strengthen us. Perhaps so, but far too often the reason we are going through such struggles is that we have chosen our own route to God's purpose and not sought and took the time and effort to know the thoughts of God.

So how do we know the thoughts of God, how can we know which is the right path to take? I believe Paul answers that in I Corinthians 2:16: "For who hath known the mind of the Lord, that he may instruct him? But we have the mind of

Christ." The word for *known* in the Greek is *egno* which comes from the word *ginosko*. This is the same word that Mary used when told she would have a child and asked how that was possible since she *knew (ginosko)* no man. *Ginosko* is an intimate knowing. No one can be intimate with God enough to *know or be intimate* with His thoughts except Jesus Christ and Paul is saying that as believers we have the *mind of Christ*. It is through Jesus Christ that we can *ginosko or be intimate* with the mind of God when we enter an intimacy with Jesus Christ. Through Jesus Christ we can *know* God's thoughts and His ways. It is through Jesus Christ who through His death and resurrection has made it possible to be intimate with Him and thus to be intimate with God and to know the thoughts of God.

Like my parents, people who have been married for many years know each other so well it is as if they can read each other's mind. No, they are not mind-readers, they just know how to read their partners. They know every little facial expression, every little movement they make. They know every gesture and idiosyncrasy. They know it so well that many times they will finish a sentence before their sweetheart finishes it. They can communicate in a way with each other that they cannot communicate with anyone else. They can do this because they *ginosko* or in the Hebrew *yada'* that is they know each other so intimately they do not even have to speak to communicate. They just know each other's mind.

People wonder how they can know the voice of God. It is no different than being married. You just have to spend time with your beloved, seek to understand their hearts, revolve your life around that person and after time you begin to ginosko or yada' intimately know that person just as you will intimately begin to know God's thoughts. God will not hold back His thoughts any more than a lover will hold back their thoughts to their beloved. But that lover will not share their thoughts with just anyone. If a wife shares her thoughts with her husband it is because he earned it, he is deserving of it, he has proven himself faithful, trustworthy and has spent considerable time with his mate to know, *ginosko, yada'* his loved one.

Years ago when I was a Junior High School teacher I used to tell my students, "You have a mind, use it." Well, as believers we have the mind of Christ, so use it. The problem with many Christians is that they are like my students, it was a lot easier for someone else to tell them the answers rather than spend time doing their homework and studying to discover the answers. They would rather someone else tell them the answers rather than use their own minds. So too with many believers, they would rather someone else tell them the mind of God rather than use the mind of Christ within them and spend time in fasting, prayer and studying the Word of God growing intimate with Him so that they will know the thoughts of God and discover His answers or directions themselves.

A husband does not want anyone else telling him what the mind of his wife is, he wants to know it first hand, and he wants her to share it with him. So too, if we love God with all our hearts, why would we want someone else to tell us what the mind of the God that we love is saying?

CHAPTER 25 – GOD'S TWINKIE

John 15:15, "Henceforth I call you not servants; for the servant knoweth not what his lord doeth: but I have called you friends; for all things that I have heard of my Father I have made known unto you."

John 12:26, "If any man serve me, let him follow me; and where I am, there shall also my servant be: if any man serve me, him will [my] Father honor."

I really enjoy driving my disability bus past our local high school at about 2:30 in the afternoon and watching the twinkies. You know what a Twinkie is, two sweet little sun yellow cakes together in a package. So you know what I am talking about. Two little scholars, a teenage boy and his steady little girlfriend holding each other's hand, staring into each other's eyes, each sharing an earplug to their iPod listening to their favorite song, so enchanted with each other, so in love they are not even aware of a big bus bearing down on them as they cross the street.

We throw the word *servant* around very loosely. We declare that we are *servants* of God, we serve God, He is our master. Yet, clearly in John 15:15 Jesus is not calling us *servants*, He is calling us *friends*. Apparently, He can't make up his mind as to whether we are His *servants* or His *friends* because just a couple chapters earlier he calls us *servants* in John 12:26.

Actually, in both the Aramaic and Greek texts two different words are used in these verses. In John 12:26 Jesus calls us his *diakone* which is one who cares for another. An appropriate word would be a *minister* or one who ministers. This would be used for a *nurse or caregiver*. The word in Aramaic *meshanamshana* also carries the same idea. In the Aramaic, this is one who voluntarily performs a service often without any pay or reward. A *meshanamshana* serves another person or a nation out of love and duty and often makes a great sacrifice in that service. Years ago there was a little song about Saint Dominic teaching that poverty was his companion and he traveled around the world never asking for a reward. He just served the Lord. That is a *meshanamashana* and that is what Jesus calls us in John 12:26.

In John 15:15 another word is used in the Greek and Aramaic but most of our modern translations still render this as a *servant*. Here the Greek word is *doulos* which is used for a *bondservant* or a *slave*. A *bondservant* is still a slave but he has voluntarily agreed to be a *slave* out of love for his master. The Aramaic word, however, is more direct. It is the word *'avad* and comes from a Semitic root word for a forced worker or laborer. This is the Aramaic word for a *slave*. A *slave* is one who must work for a master, obey the commands of a master or else he faces severe punishment or even death. Eventually, by the time of Jesus, this word *'avad* came to take on the idea of one who was obligated to obey a command. Thus, an *'avad* was also a word that was applied to a disciple. To be a disciple one had to obey every command of his master. Still one chooses to be a disciple so *'avad* evolved to mean one who would voluntarily follow a command.

This is probably why most our modern translations including the KJV use the English word *servant* for both words, as *doulos* and *diakone*, like *'avad* and *meshanamashana* tended to dovetail during the time of Jesus and were used interchangeably as the nature of slavery and servitude culturally changed. However, considering the context and our 21st-century Western concept of a *servant* and *slave*, I believe it is best that we use the English word *minister* in John 12:26, where Jesus says that if we minister to Him we will be His ministers. Again translators would balk at using the word minister (although some modern translations do use that word) because ministering to someone means meeting their needs and surely the God of the Universe who created everything could have no needs. If He needs anything He just creates it. However, there are things that even God cannot create. He cannot create a being with a free will and then command or force that person to love him because if you force someone to love you that is not love. Love's very nature is voluntary. A master cannot force a slave to love him or to perform a work out of love. This is how we can minister to God; we can give Him something that He cannot obtain on his own. God is perfect in love but he created us in His *image*. This is another tough translation because the word *image* immediately creates the idea of a physical appearance and that isn't really what the Hebrew word *tsalam* means. *Tsalam* which we render as image is really the word for *shadow or reflection*. It is a word the ancient Semites used to describe a child who resembled his father, not physically but in attitude, purpose, emotions, and behavior. We say "like father, like son" not to express the idea that the son looks like his father, but that he is behaving like his father. *Tsalam* was the ancient Semitic way of saying, "He is a chip off the old block." Hence, being made in the image of God does not mean that God has two arms, two legs eyes, ears, nose etc., it means that we are created as a reflection of God's nature which includes the ability to love. He created us because he longed to be loved by someone who would love Him voluntarily, who would choose to love Him. God can create an angel to stand by His side and say "Praise His name" but that would mean nothing more than teaching your parrot to say, "I love you." He had to give man a free will and then out of that free will man will say, "I love you." Therein is love fulfilled, that is how we can minister to God - to tell him that from the very depths of our soul and heart that we truly do love Him.

At the very root and heart of romantic love is that matter of free will. When two lovers tell each other that they are loved, the joy, the ecstasy, the cloud-9-feeling all stem from the fact that this person has chosen them out of all the people in the world to love. They feel special, they feel fulfilled and complete because someone has by an act of their free will chosen to love them. Many a story has been written about a rich young girl who is in love with a certain man. Yet that man does not love her. So her daddy wishing to make his daughter happy pays the man to spend time with her. The story continues with a joyful period of romance until the young woman finds out that the young man was paid to pretend to love her. Suddenly the whole story takes an ugly turn until the young man forsakes any money or payment to prove he loves the young woman out of his free will. It is a simple story that even a child can understand, yet why is it so hard for us to understand that being made in the image of God means that God longs for someone to love him of their own free will, not because he pays them well and keeps them out of hell but because they just freely love him even if there are no fringe benefits.

I have heard many Christians say that Jews do not believe in a heaven. I have even heard Jewish missionaries say this. I would think if someone was going to be a Jewish missionary they would study the Talmud a little for I have found that basic Judaism does teach of a heaven. Sure, like in Christianity, there is a liberal element that believes in no afterlife, but the Talmud which expresses the basis of Jewish belief does teach about an afterlife in paradise, the Garden of Eden, or Abraham's Bosom. It goes by different names but it all adds up to heaven. But why do the Jews not talk about it? I had one rabbi tell me that when they start talking about a heavenly reward, then all of a sudden you are seeking God for that reward and not seeking Him to just love Him. Every day an orthodox Jewish man will pray: "Thou shalt love the Lord thy God with all thy heart, soul, and might." Love is a daily exercise of your will. If you really seek to love God, learn to love God and practice that love, heaven will just take care of itself.

Which brings me to the next part of John 15:15, where Jesus says that he no longer calls us an *oulos (slave)* or in the Aramaic *'avad*, a slave who must serve his master under threat and intimidation, but he calls us *friends*. Here is where the Aramaic trumps the Greek. Jesus spoke in Aramaic so he did not say *philos* as we have recorded in our Greek text which simply means *brotherly love or friendship*. He calls us His *racham* His *beloved, the one He cherishes*. *Racham* is a love which is voluntarily returned, it is the love between a husband and wife, a love between two lovers who just adore each other, that is *racham*. That is what Jesus calls us, not just friends but *His beloved, the ones he cherishes*. The idea of gaining heaven and not going to hell, getting raptured to avoid seven years of tribulation, is rubbish. Heck we are so in love that if God tells us that He is rapturing everyone else but wants to keep us on earth so we can continue to share His love during those seven years of tribulation, we would consider it an honor, a privilege, nay even a joy to be able to express our love to Him in such a way.

Hey, gothic romance novels are filled with stories of rich young women who give up all their wealth to live with a man they love in poverty and they never look back to their privileged life for being with the man they love is more important than all the wealth in the world. Is it too much to assume that this kind of love can exist between God and man? It is this kind of love that God's heart is yearning for. It is this kind of love that will cause Jesus to want to go to His Father's house and prepare a place for us.

If your only reason for serving God is to escape hell and catch the tail end of the rapture, then you are no more than a *doulos* or an *'avad* (a slave). But if you can declare like the Apostle Paul, for me to live is Christ and to die is gain (Philippians 1:21) then you are His *racham,* His beloved, you are God's Twinkie.

CHAPTER 26 - LOVE (CHAV, RACHAM)

John 3:16: "For God so loved the world, that he gave his only begotten Son, that whosoever believeth in him should not perish, but have everlasting life."

John 21:20: "Then Peter, turning about, seeth the disciple whom Jesus loved following; which also leaned on his breast at supper, and said, Lord, which is he that betrayeth thee?"

We are all familiar with the three words in Greek expressing three levels of love, *Agape (unconditional love), Phileo (brotherly love, friendship)* and *Eros (erotic love)*. Hebrew actually has four words for love, but they are not always translated as love. You have *Ahav (love), Racham (tender mercies) Dodi (beloved as spousal love),* and *Ra'ah (brotherly love, or friendship)*. It would be wrong to try and make a parallel between the Greek words for love and the Hebrew words which creates a real problem in translation as *love* is at the very root and center of Scripture. I suppose we could say the closest to *Ahav* is Agape, *Ra'ah* is like *Phileo* and *Dodi* is like *Eros*. Yet this would not be accurate as *Ahav* is used in cases where *Agape* would not fit, *Ra'ah*, although rendered as friendship, is also rendered as Shepherd and consuming passion and is often used by David to express his love for God, so it would be very inappropriate to consider *Ra'ah* equivalent to *Phileo* in many cases. *Dodi* is used by Solomon toward his beloved to express a sexual desire, but it does not carry the lustful, self-gratification of *Eros*.

There is a fourth word in Hebrew for love and that is *racham* which is often expressed as a romantic love or rendered as *tender mercies*. It is rarely used in the Old Testament but is frequently found in the Aramaic New Testament where it is spelled the same and sounds the same in Aramaic as it does in Hebrew.

In the Greek New Testament, we find that the word used for *love* in John 3:16 is *Agape*. In the Peshitta or the Aramaic Bible, it is the word *Chav* which is similar to the Hebrew word *Ahav* and means *love*. However, in John 21:20 where we read about the disciple that Jesus *loved* the Greek uses the word *Agape*, but the Peshitta uses the Aramaic word *Racham* which is identical to the Hebrew word *Racham*.

We know that Jesus and His disciples did not speak in Greek, but spoke in a Northern Old Galilean dialect of Aramaic. Aramaic is very difficult to translate into another language. I believe the original manuscripts of the Gospels were written in Aramaic and translated into Greek about twenty years later, but even if I am wrong and they were originally written in Greek, the writer would still have had to translate his words and those of Jesus directly from the Aramaic. We have Aramaic manuscripts that date earlier than our earliest Greek manuscripts which were lost around 300 AD (oddly about the same time as Constantine). Still, even if Jesus and His disciples used two different Aramaic words for love, the writer and/or translator putting his words into Greek would have been stuck with only one possible word that would fit and that would be *Agape*.

So when Jesus said that "God so loved the word" He used the Aramaic word *Chav* but when speaking of the disciple that He *loved* we have the word *Racham*. These are two entirely different words, both meaning *love*. The most logical conclusion is that we are dealing with two levels of love and thus this would suggest that he either loved the world more than His disciple or he loved this disciple more than the world. In other words we face the old dilemma of Tommy Smother of the Smother brothers: "Mother always loved you best."

Is it true that God loves everyone, but He does have His favorites? Did He love Joseph more than me which is why he got to be a prime minister and I am just a bus driver for the disabled? Did God love Moses more than Miriam and Aaron which is why He spoke face to face with Moses but not with his brother or sister?

Note John 21:20 does not say the disciple whom Jesus *loved*, but the disciple whom Jesus *loved following*. In the Greek and Aramaic it is more properly rendered as the disciple whom Jesus loved *who followed Him*. The world does not follow God, but this disciple did follow Jesus.

The key difference between the words *Chav* which is used in John 3:16 as God loving the world and *Racham* as used in John 21:20 of the disciple that Jesus loved is that *Chav* is a love that is not necessarily returned. *Chav* is speaking of a love that flows from just one person and is not completed. For love to be completed, it must be returned. *Racham* is a completed love. Love can be pretty lonely and painful if it is not returned. A young teenage girl can moon over some handsome dude who doesn't even know she is alive and feel depressed, sad and broken-hearted, she can *Chav*. But if that skinny little teenage guy looks into her eyes and says: "I love you." She is immediately transported to cloud nine where birds sing and flowers look beautiful again. Love can exist if it is not returned, but it cannot sing until it is shared.

As a pastor I performed many weddings. I have always been delighted to watch *Chav* turn into *Racham* as I spoke those words: "I now pronounce you husband and wife." At that moment the reality sets in on this couple, that they have now declared to the world that they love each other and are committing their lives to each other. In that declaration they know that they are truly *loved – Racham.*

You see, God loves the world but the world does not love Him in return. It is when we love Him in return that His love is complete, it is when we love Him in return that he is able to rejoice over us with singing (Zephaniah 3:17). Salvation is not just about getting saved and going to heaven, it is about completing the love that God has for us, bringing that joy and celebration to the heart of God that has been *mooning* over us for years, like that teenage girl. Think about how He feels when you suddenly look into His eyes and say: "I love you." Why do the angels rejoice over one sinner that repents? The same reason you cry at a wedding, you are rejoicing over seeing the joy of two people (not just one) who have found each other, who share that love and return that love to each other. The angels rejoice for the same reason you read Jane Austen, Elizabeth Barrett Browning, or Grace Livingstone Hill, they love a good romance where two people love each other.

It is not that God loves one person more than the other, He loves all equally, it is just that very few will love Him in return and complete His love, bring Him the joy of His love, awaken in Him that love, and cause Him to sing with joy in that love.

You and I, simple little frail human beings, have the ability to bring joy to the God of the Universe by simply saying: "I love you." Have you told Him today that you love Him? Is God's love for you just *Chav (one sided)*? Or is it *Racham (completed, shared)*? Do you want to give the all mighty, all-powerful God a thrill and make His day? Tell Him you love Him.

CHAPTER 27 – JEALOUSY

Exodus 34:14: For thou shalt worship no other God for the Lord whose name is Jealous is a jealous God."

"O' beware my lord of jealousy, for it is the green-eyed monster which doth mock the meat it feeds upon. Shakespeare, Othello – Act 3, Scene 3.

In Shakespeare's play, Othello, Othello's servant sought to destroy his master by planting a seed of jealousy in the heart of Othello. Iago placed the handkerchief of Othello's wife, Desdemona in Cassio's, Othello's lieutenant's, room. Just a simple little thing, yet Iago knew that "trifles light as air are to the jealous confirmations strong as proofs of holy writ."

In any romantic relationship, there is one vice that is almost certain to appear, it is called jealousy. Once someone has declared their love to you and has committed themselves to love you, share their heart with you, spend their life with you, you tend to get a little possessive, you don't want to share this special love with another woman. Thus, if that lover shows the attention to someone else that you expect to receive you begin to get the feeling of jealousy.

We are taught that jealousy is bad, it is evil and leads to evil things as shown in the play Othello. Yet Scripture clearly teaches that God gets jealous. Let's examine this word jealousy from a Biblical perspective.

Renaissance man had a much different view of jealousy than we do today. That is probably why the KJV used the word *jealous* when translating the Hebrew word *quanna*. *Quanna* is used only in relationship with God. The understanding of the

English word *jealousy* has changed over the last 500 years and the understanding of the Hebrew word *quanna* more closely fits the word jealousy at the time of Shakespeare than it fits our understanding of the word today.

There are two words in the Hebrew used for jealousy, *quana* and *quanna*. There is a big difference between the two. Iago tried to make Othello understand that he was feeling *quana* and not *quanna*. *Quana* is a jealousy of envy and rage that caused Othello to be caught between the jaws of affection and anxiety. It eventually led to the tragic end of the play. Yet, Renaissance man viewed jealousy as *Quanna*. Sometimes this word is translated as *zealous*. Yet, in its Semitic root, it has the idea of a deep passion. Jealousy was something considered noble to the Renaissance man. It showed how deeply he felt toward someone. To be jealous was a good thing because it showed you were so passionate toward someone or something that you would challenge someone to a duel and die to defend your passion or honor. Such a passionate person was to be honored and trusted. Today, of course, we see that as a misdirected passion.

In the Shakespearian play, <u>Hamlet</u>, Shakespeare challenges this convention. Hamlet tells his close friend Horatio, "*Give me that man that is not passion's slave and I will wear him in my heart's core, in my heart of hearts as I do thee.*" Here Shakespeare takes a pot shot at the conventions of his day. He is challenging the notion that a deeply passionate person is to be honored and respected by saying that if one is to trust another with the very center of his heart; it is best not to do it with one who is a slave to his passion.

All that is said to shed light on what the Hebrew idea of *quanna* is. To translate *quanna* as *jealousy* is too archaic as we no longer see jealousy as a badge of honor. Probably the best translation would be *passion*. Passion still carries a positive feel to it. It is a man's passion that will cause him to lay down his life for his wife and family. It is his passion that drives him to sacrifice everything for a cause. It is his passion that causes him to perform at his best. It is God's *passion* for us that caused Him to send His Son to die on a cross. It is His passion that causes His heart to be wounded if we worship another god. Just as a wife's heart is deeply grieved and wounded if her husband worships or shows passion to another woman.

CHAPTER 28 – MAN LAYING WITH A MEMORY

Leviticus 20:13: "If a man also lie with mankind, as he lieth with a woman, both of them have committed an abomination: they shall surely be put to death; their blood [shall be] upon them."

As I was researching this book I could not help but address a passage of Scripture that is traditionally used to condemn homosexuality. I do not wish to say yea or nay on this subject but to take one of our classic Scripture passages on homosexuality and show a secondary meaning which expresses a very important matter involving a husband and wife who share an intimacy together and as a result show a subtle but important issue that we often do not address in our relationship with God.

I have always believed that homosexuality is an abomination to God, but not because of the Scriptures that are traditionally given. These Scriptures can have secondary and alternative renderings, at least from the Hebrew and Aramaic. I am not an expert in Greek so I cannot really comment on the writings of Paul which address or allegedly address this issue, however, the Aramaic version of Paul's letters could offer alternative renderings. Still, I do believe the writings of Paul were in Greek and not Aramaic so the Aramaic version is only a secondary version to be easily trumped by the Greek. So if a Greek scholar tells me that Paul is clearly addressing homosexuality in Romans 1:26-27, I Corinthians 6:9-10 and I Timothy 1:9-10 who am I to argue? I have, however, read where scholars have really questioned the traditional interpretation of these passages as homosexuality based upon a historical and cultural backdrop. But as I said, Greek and the New Testament are not my areas of expertise.

I will just leave it at that as I am not qualified to address these opposing arguments.

In the area where I have devoted my time and research, which is in the Old Testament Hebrew and Aramaic, I find there is a lot of ambiguity in the Hebrew text, I also find that most of our translations just fall in lockstep with traditional orthodoxy. I would like to just look at the problems with one particular passage. I am not saying our English Bibles have mistranslated this passage in Leviticus 20:13, I am only saying there are other avenues to explore.

Before I start, let me just say I believe homosexuality is an abomination to God because that is just not how God designed His creation. A woman is physically and emotionally different from a man and yet in such a way that she can complement a man and be a gateway for a man to understand his relationship with God and God with him. For a man to marry a man or a woman to marry a woman is diluting the picture and experience of one's relationship with God.

That being said, let me share with you an experience I had a number of years ago with a Christian friend of mine or should I say, a former friend. We had a sort of falling out over this issue of homosexuality. Let me explain. We were driving through the Viagra Triangle in downtown Chicago where the whole world seemed like a burlesque show. This former friend of mine was pointing out this woman and that woman commenting on her assets. I finally blurted out, "Enough, already. My gosh man, you're married for crying out loud!" I know I was not very tactful. But I knew his wife, a very beautiful and sweet woman, and I saw her heart was such a tender and fragile heart. I sort of insinuated that he was taking his wife, this beautiful gift from God, and trashing her with his comments. Of course, he let me know in no uncertain terms that I was not all that holy myself, which I admit he was right. However, what he said to justify himself caused me no end of unrest. He said first that she was not around and what she did not know would not hurt her. Well, come on buddy, I'm a man too and you cannot tell me that tonight when you are intimate with this gentle creature that you are not reflecting on your memory of what you were watching that afternoon. Buddy, she will know something is up. Secondly, he indicated the female body was a creation of God and his handiwork is to be admired. My thought to that was, admired yes, not compared. He had a beautiful woman at home to admire and she and she alone deserved his admiration. But then he hit me with his trump card: "Where in Scripture does it say we are not to admire the beauty of a woman?" He had me, there is a lot to say about lust, seduction, and adultery, but just to admire God's handiwork? I don't know. Perhaps that is what Leviticus 20:13 is addressing?

As I discussed this with my study partner she asked me about Leviticus 20:13 and if there were other alternative renderings. Ha, there are always alternative renderings, why do you think we have more than 110 different modern translations of the Bible? Yet, she was into some online debate going on about how to treat homosexuals and this verse was a common verse that was presented as: "See? There the Bible clearly calls homosexuality an abomination, that is what it says." Yes, that is what it says in all our modern English translations and even most of your rabbis and sages will agree that that is what it says, but not all. I fear I am one of them, one of those who march to the beat of a different drum when it comes to interpreting this verse. I share with you my thoughts, not that I am right and everyone else is wrong, not that I hold some truth. Maybe there is a Hebrew teacher out there who will point out an error I made in my translation; I will be glad to listen and will admit I am wrong if proven so.

What bothers me about this verse are the words: "*If a man also lie with mankind.*" You have two very different words for *man* and *mankind*. *Man* is *ish* and *mankind* is *zakar*. Why did it not use the word *ish* for both *man* and *mankind*? Why did it not use the word *adam* which is the word for a physical man when *ish* is the word for both a *physical* and *spiritual man*? You really have to stretch things to get *zakar* to be rendered as *mankind*. You see *zakar* means *remembrance* or *to memorialize*. We get mankind from *zakar* because we often *memorialize* man both male and female. But the idea of *zakar* is a remembrance. What is being *remembered* in this verse? The word *lie* is *shakab* which means *to crouch down, have sexual intercourse, copulate*, or *just sleep in a bed*. Literally, the verse reads, *if a man lie down with remembrance of laying with a woman the two commit an abomination.*

That does not make much sense so we must resort to paraphrasing and the most obvious paraphrase is a man lying with a man like he would do with a woman. But when I think of my former friend and how he was storing up memories, thinking of what it would be like to sleep with these women he was admiring, *if a man lie down with remembrance of laying with a woman the two commit an abomination,* begins to make sense. The two being his memories and then laying with his wife and thinking of those women. That is not only an abomination to God it is an abomination and insult to his wife, God's precious gift to him. I think this verse is addressing pornography. Then this former friend of mine had the gall to say with his nose up in the air, "Well, at least I am not a homosexual." As if that made him superior to a homosexual. Buddy, I will stand with your wife and say you are a few notches lower than a homosexual if you indulge in fantasizing about other women when sleeping with your wife.

With the ambiguity of Scripture, I find I can only approach my homosexual friends and acquaintances two ways. My simple question to them is, "If you knew beyond any doubt that Scripture clearly condemns homosexuality and you had to choose between your lifestyle and God which would you choose?" If they say they do not care about God, then I will be their friend and not condemn their lifestyle because like C.S. Lewis said, we have no right to force our morals on those who do not accept our faith. So like Jesus, I will have lunch and befriend the publicans and sinners and show them the love that Jesus showed them. Now if that person should say they would choose God over their lifestyle if they were absolutely certain it was forbidden, then I would still be their friend, for I would see them as the weaker brother who is struggling in his relationship with God and if I abandon that friendship I will one day stand in judgment before God for not helping my weaker brother.

So as far as my conscience goes, I believe homosexuality is an abomination to God, but I fear I cannot join your picket line or your hate group. I can only love them, not condemn them, pray for them and not reject them. I will only offer my outstretched hand to them in friendship, hope, and love and perhaps someday they will love the Jesus I love, and He will take care of that other issue.

But in the meantime, I will express my righteous indignation to any married man who starts gawking at another woman and then professes to be doing no harm. That wife will know something is up and God will be heartbroken over the way you handle one of his most precious gifts to you.

CHAPTER 29 – SWEET FORBIDDEN LOVE

Song of Solomon 2:3 "As the apple tree among the trees of the wood, so is my beloved among the sons. I sat down under his shadow with great delight, and his fruit was sweet to my taste."

I recall doing a study on this Song of Solomon 2:3 which indicated that the Shulamite woman was alluding to the forbidden fruit in the Garden of Eden. Commentators generally believe this is the case because the love affair between King Solomon and the Shulamite woman was a forbidden romance. Marriages were usually arranged by the fathers in those days, as they are today in many Middle Eastern countries. Love had nothing to do with a couple getting married and it was, in fact, a royal scandal to marry out of love. In some cultures, it was actually forbidden to marry out of love and in some cases it was even a capital crime to fall in love before marriage. A king would marry many wives in order to ratify a treaty with another nation. The more foreign wives a king had the more powerful he was because each wife represented his control over another nation.

Yet, no matter how strong a culture is you cannot avoid the raging hormones of a young man and woman who look at each other and hear the violins begin playing. Forget the teachings of mamma and papa, when a young girl flashes those goo goo eyes at a young man they are off in la la land regardless of how many scarves and sweaters she is wearing over her body. "It's just puppy love" has been the mother's creed since the beginning of time, but to the puppies, it is very, very real. Whether these adults will admit it or not, secretly they too can't help but enjoy a Duchess Kate and Prince William romance with a *happily ever after* ending.

Intimacy With God

Many Jewish scholars teach that the Shulamite woman was already pledged to the *Shepherd Lover* when Solomon came along. The father arranged marriages without the daughter having any say in the matter. Consider this, did we not pledge ourselves to the prince of this world and break that pledge when Jesus came along. Now we are pledged to two people, just as the Shulamite was pledged to the Shepherd Lover and then along came Solomon. One pledge had to be broken as only one man could have the Shulamite woman, just as only one person can possess us (Matthew 6:24). What is the determining factor? In ancient Jewish culture, as we see in Genesis 24:5, a woman could have a say in the matter. It was perfectly legal but morally unsound to break a pledge. Yet, it could be done especially if two men were seeking the woman's attention.

So who would the Shulamite woman pick? King or no king, if the Shulamite woman was already pledged to another man, she was still forbidden fruit to Solomon and the easiest would be to go with the *Shepherd lover*. We are already pledged to the enemy and hence we are forbidden fruit to God, the easiest would be to not upset the apple cart with any life-changing decision.

Consider too, Solomon had over 80 wives at this time; the poor *Shepherd Lover* had none. The Shulamite had a choice, she could go with the known life, the Shepherd Lover and be his only wife, or take a rare opportunity and enter a new life of the unknown and join a harem of 80 other wives and hope she will retain the affections of a king who could fall for another woman the day of the wedding, and she would risk rejection and hurt.

Verse 23 starts off a little curious: "As the apple tree among the trees of the wood so is my beloved among the sons." My study partner pointed out some time ago that the apple tree was rare in Israel at this time. Jewish literature, specifically the Midrash, points out the nub of the fruit of the apple tree emerges even before the leaves that will surround and protect the little fruit at its beginning of growth. The Midrash teaches that this symbolizes the fact the Jews were to place holy action and observance of Torah before understanding and rational acceptance. That is a holy way of saying; let your heart rule over your conventional earthly wisdom. In other words, the Shulamite woman knew that it would be safer and easier to go with the Shepherd Lover and avoid the risk of being just another woman in a harem (another tree in the forest) or to be that special apple tree and go with her heart. When the young woman says she sat under the *shadow of the apple tree with great delight (chamed – passion)* she was saying that she was making the decision based upon her heart. Both men desired her, she had to choose and she chose based on her heart. The decision was made with love. She went with her passion and she declared in the next verse that she would not be just another wife, another trophy, another foreign woman to sew up some peace or trade agreement but she would be that rare apple tree and at her wedding banquet the banner over her, the reason for this marriage would be *love*. As Tevye realized in "Fiddler on the Roof" when he found his daughter pledged to two men, it was love that made the final determination.

The young woman found that this fruit was sweet to her taste. The Qof in the word for *sweet* (Heb. *Motaq*) seals the very nature of this love relationship. Here was a king who already had 80 wives and even more concubines and he was taking on yet another wife. So just what made the Shulamite think she was so special? What is it that she had that reached the heart of this king? I want to know for that is what I need to reach the heart of my King. I think the answer is found in the word *sweet* or *motaq*. This lover found the King's fruit was sweet to her taste. I found a reference in Jewish literature that addressed the Qof in the word *motaq*: "What form of gift am I willing to offer back to the source of life in acknowledgment of all that I have taken in the course of being alive?" *Motaq* carries the idea that the sweetness was not the fruit but the smile on her beloved's face when she ate his fruit. She did not eat the fruit for her pleasure, she took pleasure in his fruit because it brought pleasure to her beloved. She knew she was special; she was that apple tree over the other wives (trees) because she brought pleasure to her beloved.

As I seek the heart of God, I find I must not seek blessings or gifts from God for my own pleasure or benefit, but if I receive a blessing from God I will take pleasure in that blessing so that God may receive pleasure from my pleasure. Even if I feel unworthy of that pleasure, I am not eating his fruit for my pleasure, I am taking pleasure in His fruit because I know it will bring pleasure to Him.

Could that have been the real issue in the Garden of Eden? Adam and Eve sought the pleasure of the fruit for their own pleasure and not the pleasure of God? They broke their pledge to God and pledged themselves to the enemy? Jesus bought us back with a dowry of His blood, but the redemption comes only when we make the choice as to which pledge to honor. It is our choice. Do we seek the known and the pleasures of this world or do we go with our passion for Him and let Him seal that pledge with His banner over us - His banner of love?

CHAPTER 30 – TENDER EYES THE REJECTED LOVER

Genesis 29:17, "Leah [was] tender eyed; but Rachel was beautiful and well favored."

We have all heard the story in Sunday School how Jacob fell in love with Leah's younger sister Rachel and agreed to work for seven years for her father Laban to purchase the rights to marry her. Then on the wedding night the old man who wanted to marry off the ugly older sister Leah secretly substituted her for her younger sister Rachel and when Jacob woke up from his wedding night he discovered he had slept with the wrong woman. Finding out the deceit involved he meekly agreed to work another seven years in order to get Rachel.

What has always baffled me is that if I were Jacob I would have hauled the old guy off to the nearest Patriarch and had the marriage annulled. If I were Rachel I would have screamed bloody murder when the preacher asked, "If there be anyone who feels this marriage should not take place speak now or forever hold your peace." Yet, it seems Rachel went along with this whole charade without as much as a peep out of her. But, like the good Christian Sunday School boy I was, I just shucked it off to one of those crazy cultural things that people engaged in those days.

But let's look at this cultural thing and especially as this story is explained in the Jewish Talmud. In Christianity, it is traditionally accepted that Jacob preferred Rachel because she was more beautiful than her sister Leah. Yet Leah was descended from Sarah who was a real knockout at the age of 90 and Leah's daughter sure did a number on the prince of Shechem, I mean this old boy was like totally smitten.

I find it hard to believe with such a glamorous gene pool that Leah turned out to be an ugly duckling. Some commentators say that the Hebrew word for *tender eyes* which is *rakak* means *to be weak* and that she had *weak* eyes. They even go on to say that this word *rakak* suggests that she really had a physical deformity and that Jacob was repulsed by her appearance. I do not find any evidence of *rakak* suggesting such a thing. Many translations such as the NIV say she had *weak* eyes, one says *ordinary* eyes, another even says *attractive* eyes, the ISV says she *looked rather plain*, another says *bleary-eyed*, and the Living Bible says there was *no sparkle in her eyes*. I say poppycock.

You trace this word *rakak* into its Semitic root, deep into the Canaanite language and you find the only concept of weakness comes from the idea that a person has such a tender heart that they could not go hunting because they could not bear to harm an innocent animal even for their own survival. Such a person was said to have *'ayani rakak* eyes *of tenderness*. This is really an ancient idiom to express the idea of a gentle, loving and caring person. It is here that I wave the KJV flag and say, "I am in your camp." Leah had *tender eyes*.

Remember Leah was the mother of Judah from whom David descended and eventually Jesus. To me the picture is almost Messianic. Leah was a caring, loving woman, the one who brought home stray cats and dogs or lambs. It is suggested that is why God blessed her with so many children because she made such a wonderful caring mother. She had so much love to give and longed for the love and affection of Jacob who just outright rejected her. Just as Jesus has so much love to give and longs for us to return that love but we just outright reject him for some physical attractiveness of this world.

In the Talmud (Bava Batra 123a) we find Judaism teaches something much different about Leah than Christianity. It is taught that because of Leah's *weak eyes* or *tenderheartedness*, she understood that one of her future children, this would be Judah, would father a great king, King David. Here is where my Christianity dovetails with the Jewish teaching. I say it was revealed in her heart that one of her future children, Judah, would be the father of the Messiah Jesus.

The Talmud teaches that she heard at the crossroads people saying, "Rebecca has two sons, and Laban has two daughters; the elder will marry the elder, and the younger will marry the younger." As she sat at the crossroads she inquired, "How does the elder one conduct himself?" They replied, "He is a wicked man, a hunter of animals." She then asked about the younger man and they said, "He is a wholesome man who cares for his mother and farms." And Leah wept until her eyelashes fell out. At that moment she was determined to marry the younger son, Jacob.

You know what I think, and this is just my opinion here, we cannot know for sure, but I would like to believe that Leah and Laban knew the destiny of the oldest child of Leah, Judah, and that child must be conceived through Jacob. We know Laban as a bad, deceitful and idolatrous man, yet maybe he had a spark of tenderness within himself and felt that his daughter Leah was such a gentle, tenderhearted and giving child that once Jacob got over his bedazzlement with the more outgoing and charming Rachel he would fall deeply in love with Leah and forget all about Rachel. I would like to think he had Jacob work seven years for Rachel in the hope that he would see the real beauty in Leah and decide to marry her and failing in that maybe another seven years as the husband to Leah he would discover she was his true love which unfortunately never happened.

Rachel's son Joseph may have gotten top billing but ultimately the tribe of Joseph is never mentioned among the twelve tribes and is believed to have been absorbed into the tribes of Ephraim and Manasseh, we just are not sure. The tribe of Benjamin, Rachel's other son nearly got wiped out and were known as the warring tribe. Judah, however, was the son through which Jesus came. Judah was the eldest, he should have received the birthright that Jacob was bestowing upon Joseph, he should have had the coat of many colors, yet it was Judah who stood up for Joseph when the other brothers wanted to kill him. It was Judah who saved Joseph's life. Judah was his mother's son, tender-hearted.

The point is, I like to think that my Jesus descended from a mother who was not a bleary-eyed, ordinary eyed, weak-eyed, plain looking woman who had no sparkle in her eye. I like to think that my Savior descended from a tender-hearted, loving woman with a sparkle in her eyes who took in lost sheep, cats, and puppies and just really got a bum rap.

CHAPTER 31 – THE MOST PRECIOUS THING

Job 13:15 "Though he slay me, yet I will trust in Him."

In the Hebrew, this affirmation of Job is much stronger than it appears in English, although it appears you cannot get much stronger than this. Yet, by translating the word *hen* as *though* it comes across as *"even if he does."* But the word *hen* is often translated as *Behold*. The word for *slay me* is *yeketeleni* which is in a simple Qal imperfect form. In others words, you would be correct to translate this as *Behold* or *"Surely, he will slay me."* The root word for *slay* is *qatal* which is used only three times in the Old Testament. This is not your usual word for kill which would be *ratsach* for *murder* or *harag* for *manslaughter* all of which refer to a *physical killing*. *Qatal* can mean not only a physical killing but it also means a killing of the spirit. It is also a killing of all hope. It also means to *make small*, or be*little value.*

It is very interesting the writer uses the word *qatal* here. We can boldly say like Job, *though he does the worst to me I will still trust him.* But Job takes it one step further in his use of this word. Though he breaks every promise, fails me in every way, treats me like I am a worthless piece of @#%&, I am still going to trust in Him. The word used for *trust* here is also an unusual word. It is *yachal* which means to have an *expectant hope*. You see Job fully expected to die, the use of the Qal imperfect implies that God is going to take his life, it is not an *if* situation. Job is saying that when God takes his life, he will be hoping and expectantly waiting to be with God.

Raised as a Baptist, I was well trained in the art of evangelism. In fact, I remember sitting in evangelistic classes being taught by a successful salesman from the secular world how to market God. You first establish the person's need for the product. Then you demonstrate how the product works, often through testimonials, then you show how your product meets your client's need, and of course, you get them to sign on the dotted line (sinner's prayer) and bingo, you wrapped up another sale. Of course, if the product doesn't work, there is no refund. We sold God as a means to an end, but not as someone you can love and hope to be with one day.

If Job signed on the dotted line with God for all the benefits, he surely would have been seeking a refund. How many of us cling to the promises of God and yet, it just doesn't seem like He is fulfilling these promises. What happens if He doesn't fulfill them? It is easy to love Him when He gives wonderful promises and keeps them. Would you still love Him if He broke His promises? We cannot help but love Him when preachers tell us how much He loves us and how we are the center of His world. But suppose He *qatals* us or makes us feel like we are worthless, would we still love Him? This is what Job is saying, He will still trust or *yachal* God. He will still continue to hope and place his life and future in the hands of God even if God treats him like he is worthless and never fulfills His promise.

Job's relationship with God did not depend upon all the benefits. Without fail when I speak of the Book of Job some Christian will always say: "Yeah, but remember, once Job came through it all, God restored everything and more to him." To say that means you missed the whole point of the book. That restoration part is an epilogue, it is not a part of the story or the theme of the story. It is just information that is added at the end, separate from the story and not intended to take away from the theme of the story. The theme of the story of Job is that when it was all taken away and it seemed like his life was going to end in poverty and shame, he was still *yachal* was waiting and hoping expectantly to be with the God he loved.

There is a story in Jewish literature about a married man who longed to be single again and not be burdened with a wife. One day he learned that under Jewish law he could divorce his wife if she did not give him a child after ten years of marriage. The man had found his escape as the couple was childless, not that he really cared or tried. Yet, it was a loophole that he would seize. He went to the rabbi and demanded that the rabbi grant a divorce based upon this Jewish law. The rabbi knew this couple and said he would grant the divorce only after speaking to the man's wife. After meeting with the man's wife he called him to his office and told him he would grant the divorce under one condition. The man was crestfallen, he knew there was a catch. Yet, the rabbi explained that the one condition was that he would allow his wife to go into his house and pick out the one thing that was the most precious thing to her and he was to let her have it. The man's apprehensions turned to joy. "That's it? That is all? Just let her have the one thing that is most precious to her? I'm free!" He then ran out into the streets and grabbed his drinking buddies and that night had a big party to celebrate his new freedom. Unfortunately, the old boy made a little too merry and soon passed out in a drunken stupor. When he awoke he found himself in bed in his father-in-law's house with his wife sitting next to him. He looked around and saw his wife and asked what he was doing there. His wife replied, "The rabbi said I could go to your house and take what was most precious to me." The man brightened up and asked? "Did you find it?" She said, "Yes, it was you." The story goes that the man did not get the divorce but remained contentedly married to his wife.

Sometimes, like with Job, God has to allow everything to be taken away from us so we can discover what it is that is really most precious to us. It is then we discover it is something that not even the enemy, nor any human, nor death, nor life, nor angels, nor principalities, nor powers, nor things present, nor things to come, nor height, nor depth, nor any other creature, shall be able to separate us from: and that is the love of God, which is in Christ Jesus our Lord. (Romans 8).

CONCLUSION

I can sum up this whole book by saying that if you want to understand what the love of God is like, how to express the love of God and how the experience the love of God, then look at the marriage relationship as God intended the marriage relationship to be. A relationship where a man and woman join together in intimacy, in sharing their hearts, in sharing their lives, in including their mates in every aspect of their lives and in growing deeper and deeper in love until they can almost read each other's minds until they know the meaning behind each little gesture their mate makes. That is how our relationship with God is meant to be. When we accept Jesus as our personal Savior that begins our betrothal period of learning to love this God who gave His Son so He could have an intimate relationship with us.

There is just one other aspect to this relationship that I did not mention. It is the backslider, or the husband or wife who wanders away, who repents and returns. I spoke with a man who had been an alcoholic, stolen from his wife and child to support his addition. He was brutal with his family and soon left them in poverty, to wander the streets of a major city. One day he wandered into a mission and as he told it he "heard the Gospel." He came back and "heard the Gospel." He returned and this time he heard the Gospel. He entered into a betrothal with Jesus and Jesus began to clean up his life. He longed to return to his wife and child but felt he had burnt too many bridges and they would not want him back. Yet, through the encouragement of the mission director and his pastor, he was reunited with his wife and child. His wife is a very sweet lady who forgave him and loved him and they worked together in the inner city of Washington DC for many years directing a mission to help others find this amazing love. If a woman who has been abused, humiliated and treated as horribly as this woman could forgive her husband, how much more can the Father in heaven forgive us?

There is a story in the Talmud of a king who could not get along with his son. The disagreements were such that the son left his father's kingdom to live in another kingdom. After some time the father sent a messenger to his son asking: "Would you come home?" The son sent the message back that it was just too far to travel. The father returned the messenger with this message, "Then come as far as you can, and I will meet you."

The Bible says in James 4:8: *"Draw nigh to God and he will draw nigh to you."* Note who has to make the first move. It is us. We are the offending party, we are the ones who left a broken-hearted lover, it is we who must make that first move. But if we do and go as far as we can, He will meet us to take us the rest of the way.

As a child, I remember accepting Jesus as my Savior and experiencing the joy of this new found love. Before love, however, I began listening to preachers who seemed to indicate I just did not accept Jesus the right way. I did not say that sinner's prayer the right way, I was not really sorry for my sins and of course, if you are not sorry for your sins you cannot repent so I felt I really did not repent. I prayed the sinners' prayer over and over, never feeling like I was saved. I tried to feel sorry for my sins but I just could not work up that grief that I was supposed to have. I began to despair that I would go to hell and there was just nothing I could do about it.

Then one day I read a Question and Answer book by a famous preacher who answered a question from a person who had the same problem I had. His answer was this: "God wants you a million times more than you want Him."

I realize today that when I accepted Jesus into my life, I entered a betrothal, a marriage with Him. He married me because He loved me and He wants me as His companion a million times more than I want Him. But like any lover, I have to learn to trust in that love and that love will endure any wrongs against it.

You may have noticed that I did not include anything in this book about divorce. The reason is Isaiah 50:1: "Thus saith the LORD, Where [is] the bill of your mother's divorcement, whom I have put away? Or which of my creditors [is it] to whom I have sold you? Behold, for your iniquities have ye sold yourselves, and for your transgressions is your mother put away."

There is one thing we can be sure of in our betrothal/marriage with God, He will not divorce. No matter how much we may break His heart or sin we will never have to fear an angel appearing at our door with a bill of divorcement.

Chaim Bentorah All Access
HebrewWordStudy.com

Just imagine, having all this at your fingertips, on demand:

- More than 1000 Hebrew studies
- Hebrew Alphabet poster (download)
- Online Hebrew Course
- Learning God's Love Language audio
- Learning God's Love Language
- Learning God's Love Language Workbook
- For Whom My Soul Loves: $7.99 value
- Through the Daleth: $7.99 value
- The Healing Presence of God
- God's Heart in the Marriage Relationship
- The Heart of God in Praise and Worship
- Psalm 91: Deliverance From Fear
- God's Love For Us
- Weekly live-stream teaching
- 24/7 access: "Ask Chaim"
- Video Hebrew word studies
- Free Hebrew Alphabet video teaching
- 20% off insider discount on Chaim Bentorah books.
- and much more – this just keeps growing!

Visit: www.HebrewWordStudy.com

About the Author

Chaim Bentorah is the pseudonym of a Gentile Christian who taught college-level Biblical Hebrew and is an Amazon Bestselling Author. He prepared his students to take the placement exams for graduate school. He has now developed a method of study where he can prepare any Believer, regardless of age or academic background, to study the Word of God using Biblical Hebrew.

Chaim Bentorah received his B.A. degree from Moody Bible Institute in Jewish Studies and his M.A. degree from Denver Seminary in Old Testament and Hebrew and his PhD in Biblical Archeology. His Doctoral Dissertation was on the "Esoteric Structure of the Hebrew Alphabet." He has taught Classical Hebrew at World Harvest Bible College for thirteen years and also taught Hebrew for three years as a language course for Christian Center High School. He is presently teaching Biblical Hebrew and Greek to pastors in the Metro Chicago area.

www.chaimbentorah.com

Other books by Chaim Bentorah

- Learning God's Love Language
- Learning God's Love Language Workbook
- Hebrew Word Study: Revealing The Heart Of God
- Journey into Silence: Transformation Through Contemplation, Wonder, and Worship
- For Whom My Soul Loves: A Hebrew Teacher's Journey to Understanding God's Love
- Hebrew Word Study: Ancient Biblical Words Put into a Modern Context with the Help of the People Who Ride My Bus
- Is This Really Revival?
- Biblical Truths From Uncle Otto's Farm

Printed in Great Britain
by Amazon